Palgrave Studies of Entrepreneurship and Social Challenges in Developing Economies

Series Editor
Rajagopal
EGADE Business School
Tecnológico de Monterrey
Mexico City, Mexico

This series explores the role of entrepreneurship in managing social challenges comprising poverty, gender inequality, sustainability and climate change, income disparity, social healthcare, community housing and homelessness, and clean food and water supplies across Asia, Africa, and Latin America.

Entrepreneurship in developing countries has an economic motivation and it is taken up as a survival occupation. The books in this series discuss various attributes of social enterprises, innovation, technology, and the role of leadership in meeting the recurring social challenges. The discussion on entrepreneurship in this book series is central to social entrepreneurship, family enterprises, entrepreneurial business models, disruptive innovation, consumer behavior, marketing-mix, branding, profit and performance, market expansion, new product development, operations and supply chain, manufacturing, and servitization. In addition, the volumes in this book series also address the PESTEL (political, economic, social, technological, environmental, and legal) perspectives that support socio-economic development.

Rajagopal • Ananya Rajagopal

Artificial Intelligence and Entrepreneurship

Enhancing Competitiveness and Innovation in Emerging Markets

palgrave
macmillan

Rajagopal
EGADE Business School
Tecnológico de Monterrey
Mexico City, Mexico

Ananya Rajagopal
Facultad de Economia y Negocios
Universidad Anáhuac México
Ciudad De Mexico, Mexico

ISSN 2731-6874 ISSN 2731-6882 (electronic)
Palgrave Studies of Entrepreneurship and Social Challenges in Developing Economies
ISBN 978-3-032-14903-9 ISBN 978-3-032-14904-6 (eBook)
https://doi.org/10.1007/978-3-032-14904-6

This Palgrave Macmillan imprint is published by the registered company Springer Nature Switzerland AG.
The registered company address is: Gewerbestrasse 11, 6330 Cham, Switzerland

With love to
Arati
Akhilesh, and
Niharika

Acknowledgments

Entrepreneurship and enterprise development have been contemporary topics which have triggered a potential marketing approach to be explored while Professor Rajagopal was teaching courses on E-commerce Management, and Innovation and Global Competitiveness at Boston University. The core engagement of Professor Rajagopal in organizing first-in-series, the International Symposium on Entrepreneurship and Technology at Metropolitan College, Boston University, since 2023, has induced new insights into developing socio-economic and technology models to improve entrepreneurship in developing countries. Such impetus has evolved discussion on game-changer models in this book. Professor Rajagopal sincerely thanks Dr. Tanya Zlateva, Dean, Metropolitan College of Boston University for giving me opportunity to teach related subjects, which enabled me to meticulously develop and apply research-based learning on technology-led entrepreneurship and business modeling in the classes. Discussions with Dr. Vladimir Zlatev, Associate Professor of Practice at Administrative Sciences Department, Metropolitan College, Boston University, have also benefited the horizon of knowledge on the subject immensely. Discussions with Dr. Irena Vodenska, Department Chair, and Dr. Marcus Goncalves, Associate Chair of the Department, on this topic also enriched the contents of this book.

Professor Rajagopal would like to acknowledge the support of Dr. Horacio Arredondo, Dean, EGADE Business School, and Dr. Lucila Osorio, Director, Marketing and Business Intelligence Department of EGADE Business School, who have always encouraged him to take up new challenges in teaching graduate courses, develop new insights, and contribute to the existing literature prolifically. He thanks all his students of graduate and doctoral programs at EGADE Business School for sharing enriching ideas on the subject during the classroom discussions, which helped in building this book on the framework of innovative ideas.

Ananya Rajagopal expresses sincere thanks to Jose Rodrigo Pozón López, Vice rector (Academic), Rebeca Iliana Arevalo Marinez (Research Director), and Edgar González Olea, Dean of Business and Economics Division at Anahuac University, Mexico, for the encouragement to take up new research endeavors. She has been significantly educated by the comments and suggestions of various anonymous referees on her previous research work related to entrepreneurship, innovation, and marketing strategy that helped her in developing this contribution.

We express sincere thanks to Marcus Ballenger, Commissioning Editor, Scholarly Business, Palgrave Macmillan, for encouraging me to work on this research and accepting the proposal for publication. We are thankful to various anonymous referees of our previous research works on entrepreneurship, innovation, and technology management that helped us in looking deeper into the conceptual gaps and improving the quality with their valuable comments. Though it was a challenging journey with this publication project from ideation to manuscript preparation, we must acknowledge the encouragement from senior academics to proceed ahead with the project. We express our deep gratitude to Arati Rajagopal, who always reminded us of this task over other deadlines on the agenda. She also deserves kudos for copy editing the manuscript rigorously before submitting it to the publisher.

Praise for *Artificial Intelligence and Entrepreneurship*

"Synergy of artificial intelligence (AI) and machine learning (ML) is infinite, leveraging intelligence to foster entrepreneurship. AI and ML concept is much talked in crowd but less explored by the entrepreneurs…This book dissects every aspect of transcending technology that impacts the new horizon of entrepreneurship. A good read for everyone…"

—Rebeca-Illiana Arévalo-Martínez, PhD, *Research Director, Universidad Anáhuac México*

"With the manifold impact of AI, the only way for entrepreneurs to get out of a tight box is to adapt to the technology ecosystem…with the progressing AI, world is summoning the future and entrepreneurs are not far behind…flowing with concurrence, this book bridges a plethora of new concepts on AI and ML connecting entrepreneurs to platform skills and business modeling with examples and case studies…an enriching contribution and a timely book for all…"

—Neil Hernández Gress, PhD, *Director for Research, Tecnologico de Monterrey, Mexico*

Contents

Part III Navigation Ahead

About the Authors

Rajagopal is Distinguished Professor of Marketing at EGADE Business School of Tecnologico de Monterrey (ITESM), at Mexico City Campus, and Fellow of the Royal Society for Encouragement of Arts, Manufacture and Commerce, London. He is Fellow of the Chartered Management Institute and Fellow of Institute of Operations Management, United Kingdom. He has been visiting professor at Boston University, Boston, Massachusetts, since 2013. Dr. Rajagopal is also visiting professor since August 2020 at the UFV India Global Education of the University of the Fraser Valley, Canada, and teaches marketing-related courses. He has been listed with biography in various international directories.

Dr. Rajagopal holds post-graduate and doctoral degrees in Economics and Marketing respectively from Pandit Ravishankar Shukla University in India. His specialization is in the field of Marketing Management. He has to his credit 83 books on marketing management and rural development themes, and over 450 research contributions that include published research papers in national and international refereed journals. He is Editor-in-Chief of *International Journal of Leisure and Tourism Marketing* and *International Journal of Business Competition and Growth*. Dr. Rajagopal has been Associate Editor of *Emerald Emerging Markets Case Studies* (2012–19), published by Emerald Publishers, United Kingdom. He is on the editorial board of various journals of international repute.

Dr. Rajagopal has been conferred the honor of distinguished professor by the EGADE Business School, Mexico, in 2020. His research contributions have been recognized by the Ministry of Science, Humanities, Technology, and Innovation, Government of Mexico, by awarding him the highest level of National Researcher-SNI Level-III in 2013. He has been awarded UK-Mexico Visiting Chair 2016–17 for collaborative research on 'Global-Local Innovation Convergence' with University of Sheffield, United Kingdom, instituted by the Consortium of Higher Education Institutes of Mexico and the United Kingdom. Dr. Rajagopal has been conferred the Overseas Indian Award (*Pravasi Bhartiya Samman Award*) in January 2023 for his outstanding contribution in the field of Education. This is the highest honor conferred by the President of India.

Ananya Rajagopal is Research Professor at Universidad Anáhuac Mexico. She holds a PhD in Administration with focus on Entrepreneurship and Marketing Strategies from EGADE Business School, Tecnológico de Monterrey. She obtained her Master of Business Administration (MBA) degree from Alliant International University, San Diego, specializing in Strategic Management. She has obtained two Bachelor of Science degrees: BS in Industrial and Systems Engineering from the Tecnológico de Monterrey, and BS in International Business Administration from Alliant International University, San Diego. She has ample experience in the financial industry in Mexico City since 2006. She has been conferred the Level II membership of National System of Researchers (SNI-Level II) of Ministry of Science, Humanities, Technology, and Innovation, Government of Mexico.

Ananya Rajagopal has published several papers in international journals of repute and contributed research works in international conferences and edited books. Ananya Rajagopal is author of the five books comprising *Managing Startup Enterprises in Emerging Markets: Leadership Dynamics and Marketing Strategies*, *Epistemological Attributions to Entrepreneurial Firms: Linking Organizational Design and Operational Efficiency*, *Women Entrepreneurs in Emerging Markets: Managing Performance within Ecosystems*, *Towards Cleaner Entrepreneurship: Bridging Social Consciousness and Sustainability*, and *Unmasking Invisible Challenges in Entrepreneurship: Five Game Changer Models*. She is reviewer of several journals of international repute including *Emerald Emerging Markets Case Studies*, *Journal of Transnational Management*, and *Journal of Strategy and Management*. She is also a member of the advisory panel of Elsevier Insights. Ananya Rajagopal is member of the editorial board of *Humanities and Social Science Communications* journal (Springer Nature). She has presented her research in high order professional international bodies including Academy of Management, Academy of Marketing Science, and Association for Consumer Research.

List of Figures

CHAPTER 1

Preface

Continuous evolution of information and communication technologies (ICT) has significantly driven digitalization of conventional business processes and the Internet of Things (IoT) concept in business. The competitive engagement of firms with virtual technologies tends to unveil new business models (BMs) within hybrid environments. This phenomenon has extensively contributed to the continuous growth of the new business economy in a hybrid environment. Such business impetus is developed around the so-called metaverses. In the cyber-physical ecosystem, BMs have been developed as a combination of physical- and virtual-world mechanisms that help in developing social and economic values. Reviewing changing technological perspectives, Artificial Intelligence (AI) is often considered the 'fifth wave' of computing, signifying a major transformative technological advancement that is currently shaping various industries and aspects of life, characterized by autonomous AI systems capable of operating independently in complex environments.[1] Economic creation and value capture at the crossroads of physical and virtual economies today are enabled through the cyber revolution comprising AI, AR, VR, and

[1] Kim, R. Y. (2024). The Fifth Wave: The Sustainability Age and New Industrial Revolution, in *IEEE Engineering Management Review*, 1–12. DOI: https://doi.org/10.1109/EMR.2024.3379036

Rajagopal, A. Rajagopal, *Artificial Intelligence and Entrepreneurship*, Palgrave Studies of Entrepreneurship and Social Challenges in Developing Economies,
https://doi.org/10.1007/978-3-032-14904-6_1

metaverse. BMs based on digital technologies and within hybrid environments are becoming increasingly popular to facilitate innovative products and services offerings, collaborations, and transactions through new interaction modalities within community-based and crowd-based contexts. Therefore, virtual BMs are challenging and innovating the traditional market dynamics which not only augments profit, but also helps in managing unforeseen business conditions. Consequently, firms implementing virtual business models have been successful in reducing the cost, time, and risk factors in business and enhancing market-oriented innovations in digital and virtual environments.

An innovative technology that, by its superior attributes, can change the way consumers, industries, or businesses operate, is called disruptive technology, and it refers to a set of innovative technologies behind Industry 4.0 that can change the way people work. Disruptive technology in the smart tourism industry can become successful and effective through synchronous AR/VR connectivity and many transmission capabilities. Companies must use sophisticated mathematical models and analysis programs to enable AR/VR to accurately represent every physical movement and feature of the online tourists in real time. Advanced cloud computing is another key factor that makes AR/VR disruptive technology. AR/VR must instantly embed attractions, virtual-physical integration, somatosensory manipulation, and active monitoring of online tourists' dynamic behavior to be able to create a highly immersive and smooth experience. However, strong support of advanced cloud computing, image processing, Big Data, AI, and Internet of Things is needed to do this.

Entrepreneurship and the emergence of AI have created new dimensions in entrepreneurial operations and business modeling. The synchronization of AI with entrepreneurship has grown from a public perspective, which is encouraged by government, corporations, and entrepreneurial groups to develop platform-oriented businesses using advanced technologies. However, micro, small, and medium entrepreneurs are yet to reach the core of AI and develop convergence with the advanced knowledge provided by AI with the existing practices. Such gap often challenges the synchronization of AI with entrepreneurship by streamlining the obscure knowledge to outperform the entrepreneurial business against conventional odds. Consequently, AI-based entrepreneurship throws various challenges in micro, small, and medium enterprises at various stages of their growth. In this context, this book critically analyzes the effect of AI on entrepreneurial performance by transforming the obscure knowledge on technology to enable enterprises to stay competitive by integrating the triadic course of innovation, technology, and business.

Entrepreneurial decision making conventionally depends on knowledge derived from experience, cognitive analysis, and intellectual bandwidth of entrepreneurs, which tends to synchronize metacognition and meta-learning in developing entrepreneurial competitiveness.[2] AI-based knowledge tends to move entrepreneurs' competence from the obscure processes to technology-led competitiveness. However, entrepreneurial trust is the key moderator in bridging cognitive obscurity with technology-led competitiveness utilizing the AI and ML platforms. In this process, AI and ML inflict several cognitive challenges and undisclosed operational conflicts.[3] Acquiring knowledge through AI resources helps in building real-time knowledge repositories, but deriving decisions out of these knowledge pools often create task-level disagreements and conflicts with conventional operational processes. A wide range of semantics is generated by AI and ML platforms, which offers numerous options to make entrepreneurial decisions and create cognitive spirals and reconstructs the experience-based entrepreneurial processes. Consequently, adapting to AI- and ML-based suggestions have intrinsic and extrinsic challenges due to weak reasoning capabilities of entrepreneurs who are new learners of AI and ML knowledge streams.[4] The global awareness on technology-conscious entrepreneurship has increased the demand for innovative and technology friendly products across countries. Consequently, technology-entrepreneur interface has shifted toward AI- and ML-driven entrepreneurial, manufacturing, and services markets. Entrepreneurs are cautious about developing AI- and ML-based enterprises that cater to contemporary market needs and play a significant role in reshaping the entrepreneurial ecosystem. However, the concept of AI-driven entrepreneurship is at an infant stage, and it involves economic and technological

[2] Sturm, T., Pumplun, L., Gerlach, J.P., Kowalczyk, M., and Buxmann, P. (2023). Machine learning advice in managerial decision-making: The overlooked role of decision makers' advice utilization. *The Journal of Strategic Information Systems*, 32(4), https://doi.org/10.1016/j.jsis.2023.101790.

[3] Fügener, A., Grahl, J., Gupta, A., and Ketter, W. (2021). Will Humans-in-the-Loop Become Borgs? Merits and Pitfalls of Working With AI. *MIS Quarterly*, 45(3), 1527–1556.

[4] Wang, S., Noe, R.A., and Wang, Z. (2014). Motivating knowledge sharing in knowledge management systems. *Journal of Management*, 40(4), 978–1009.

complexities.[5] In these entrepreneurial dynamics, the trust factor in AI and ML is ambidextrous, which often creates conflicts among the user perceptions and minimizes the possibilities of quick adaptability to technology and advanced management practices.[6]

Most researchers have expressed that AI-based entrepreneurship is a big part of the rise of a new industry. Creation of the technology-led market brings about both economic growth and environmental improvement. Emerging enterprises design and implement AI- and ML-based programs as pragmatism. These enterprises have consistently generated significant growth rates and profit margins with the technology-based programs irrespective of their size and destination. The pursuit of AI in entrepreneurship, therefore, has emerged as a powerful path to grow entrepreneurial businesses. Review of the current trend and success of the AI- and ML-supported enterprises of micro, small, and medium level has significantly impacted the problem-solving scenarios through AI- and ML-led designing and quality function deployment, narrowing down the tradeoffs between complexity and accuracy in decision making in improving the entrepreneurial behavior.[7]

The use of AI in various entrepreneurial activities including designing, manufacturing, and marketing is expanding rapidly at the bottom of the pyramid.[8] This philosophy gained increasing importance in the AI-led entrepreneurship, which supports diverse and inclusive innovation driven by technology platforms, which have pioneered small-scale innovations within emerging economies. Technology-based entrepreneurship has emerged as a competitive strategy for innovation to make the enterprises competitive and co-create entrepreneurial innovation by engaging the stakeholders. Consequently, technology-based entrepreneurship focused

[5] Gupta, M. and Dharwal, M. (2022). Green entrepreneurship and sustainable development: A conceptual framework. *Materials Today: Proceedings*, 49 (8), 3603–3606.

[6] Zhu, H., Chen, Z., and Liu, S. (2023). Learning knowledge representation with meta knowledge distillation for single image super-resolution. *Journal of Visual Communication and Image Representation*, Vol. 95, https://doi.org/10.1016/j.jvcir.2023.103874

[7] Sustacha, I., Baños-Pino, J.F., and Del Valle, E. (2023). The role of technology in enhancing the tourism experience in smart destinations: A meta-analysis. *Journal of Destination Marketing & Management*, Vol. 30, https://doi.org/10.1016/j.jdmm.2023.100817

[8] Brugmann, J. and Prahalad, C.K. (2007). Cocreating Business's New Social Compact. *Harvard Business Review*, 85 (2), 80–90.

on developing innovative products and inculcating technology consciousness for entrepreneurial business growth.[9]

In view of the above discussion, the book focuses on divergent discussions on entrepreneurial challenges in context to the adaptation to AI-based technological environment comprising machine learning, robotics, and large language modeling (LLM) to enhance entrepreneurial knowledge and scope of decision making. This book discusses technological intervention in contemporary entrepreneurial practices concerning manufacturing, operations, innovation, and marketing in micro, small, and medium enterprises. Discussions across chapters analyze critical factors affecting the success and failure of enterprises adapting to the AI, ML, and LLM convergent models, which supports global-local business paradigm. While analyzing the critical factors, the challenges in converging technology-based entrepreneurial models with conventional practices have been categorically focused across the chapters by exhibiting semantic mapping. The book also discusses developing technology-based entrepreneurial models connecting the manufacturing, marketing, and services platforms for integrated economic development in developing economies.

The convergence of entrepreneurship and technology enables micro, small, and medium enterprises to gain competitive advantage in the marketplace by driving tactical moves. Sometimes such small changes in these enterprises introduced through innovation and technology in the niche markets drive macro effects in large markets. This phenomenon can be explained as the butterfly effect and has been discussed in the articles included in this book. Often, strategic choices of micro, small, and medium enterprises lean toward developing competitive differentiations that enable consumers to realize value for money and loyalty moves in the competitive marketplace. Such consumer perceptions may have a large impact on market share and profitability. How start-up enterprises can be benefitted through the collective intelligence in managing open innovations at low-cost (frugal innovation) and 'refresh' consumer value with small changes with differentiation (radical approach) and marketing policy to gain larger, sustainable, and competitive advantage is explained in the book.[10] There

[9] Chavez, M.R., Butler, T.S., Rekawek, P., Heo, H., and Kinzler, W.L. (2023). Chat generative pre-trained transformer: why we should embrace this technology. *American Journal of Obstetrics and Gynecology*, 228 (6), 706–711.

[10] Haigh, N., Walker, J., Bacq, S., & Kickul, J. (2015). Hybrid organisations: Origins, strategies, impacts, and implications. *California Management Review*, 57 (3), 5–12.

are many embedded technical and organizational aspects that affect managerial decision making by utilizing the AI and ML platforms. The managerial trust is largely affected by the choice spread and overload in decision making while resolving the organizational problems at various levels. Though AI and ML offer great potential to craft managerial decisions by augmenting the verbal and non-verbal data, influence in decision making requires total quality assessment and transparency at various levels of decisions.[11]

As the competition among firms in the marketplace across the territory and market segments is perennially growing, the butterfly effect has become much more dispersed, complexity in market predictions has increased, and tactical interventions have turned to business models involving consumers and social media in demonstrating effects on larger scale. Innovative and disruptive enterprises successfully operating in the global-local marketplace need to overcome the organizational barriers and transaction costs involved with innovation, technology application, and managing intellectual property besides developing effective production, operations, and marketing strategies.[12] Firms must also evaluate how best to appropriate value to innovations and technology interventions within the organization and marketplace. The discussions in this book harness the power of firms toward sensitive market interventions through marketing-mix strategies, innovation, and technology applications to click larger effects with smaller differentiations. Consequently, advancement in technology has become a crucial component in building organizational cognition to support technology-based decision making among managers. Technology, organizational structure, and ecosystem of managerial decision making are three domains needed to facilitate agile working environment and promote inter-disciplinary collaboration to streamline the multi-layered decision making and improve operational efficiency in enterprises.[13]

[11] Coombs, C., Hislop, D., Taneva, S.K., and Barnard, S. (2020). The Strategic Impacts of Intelligent Automation for Knowledge and Service Work: An Interdisciplinary Review. *Journal of Strategic Information Systems*, 29 (4), 1–30.

[12] Rajagopal (2015). *Butterfly Effect in Competitive Markets: Driving Small Change for Larger Differences*. Basingstoke, UK: Palgrave Macmillan.

[13] Vogelsang, K., Liere-Netheler, K., Packmohr, S., and Hoppe, U. (2018). Success factors for fostering a digital transformation in manufacturing companies. *Journal of Enterprise Transformation*, 8 (1–2), 121–142.

Differentiators

This book explores the brighter side of advanced technologies against the darker sides of conventional wisdom, which is supported by Artificial Intelligence and machine learning to drive entrepreneurial competitiveness in the changing business ecosystem. This book analyzes the chronological growth in technology and the nexus between AI and entrepreneurship to harness the power of technology. The book also discusses the conjunction of technology and the human factor by analyzing the AI wealth and shifts in the human mind explained by A4 factors comprising awareness, attributes, affordability, and adaptability. AI at the grassroots has been defined as the fifth wave, which explains the chronological development of co-intelligence of human mind and machines. The overall discussions in the book categorically blend the business modeling in the AI ecosystem encapsulating tangible (data mining, data analytics, and AI-based decisions) and intangible factors (entrepreneurial appraisal, knowledge management, and emotional modeling). Navigating into the future, the book optimistically discusses the changing cyberscape[14] with the growth of cloud technology, LLM and metaverse, which tends to affect all development sectors within the macro entrepreneurship perspectives.

Debates Engaged

This book discusses how chronological growth in technology has transformed entrepreneurial knowledge and skills to harness diverse perspectives of Artificial Intelligence and machine learning. Discussion across chapters engages critical debate on synchronizing AI and human factors to converge conventional wisdom and the growing AI wealth. The debate on the contemporary synergy between technology and the human factor is conducted by analyzing the A4 factors and the semantics of entrepreneurial mind in nurturing new designs and managing innovative disruption. The arguments on vulnerable topics of AI-led business modeling are supported by entrepreneurial cases on products and services management. An out-of-the-box debate is engaged on the fifth wave entrepreneurial business by mapping chronologically the evolution of fifth wave, which comprises the entrepreneurial growth across the stages—social entrepreneurship,

[14] The virtual landscape of the cyberspace.

niche business entrepreneurship, cooperative entrepreneurship, local-global entrepreneurship, and entrepreneurial business models based on digital, hybrid, and AI-based platforms. The book opens arguments on sematic methods for business processes, emotional modeling, and data-based decision making to make enterprises competitive and profitable. At the core, the discussions intertwine the AI adaptability and the entrepreneurial transformation and present arguments on the changing cyberscape and growing AI intervention in entrepreneurship. The book also debates on the changing risk management practices in enterprise planning while adapting to AI, ML, LLM, metaverse, and Internet of Things (IoT).

Benefits Offered by the Contents, Scope, and Organization of the Book

This book provides a contemporary platform for readers to understand the impact of AI technology on entrepreneurship and planning micro, small, and medium enterprises by engaging with technological transformations. Accordingly, this book offers innovative, applied, and valuable content by validating the core and peripheral debates with focus on decision making in enterprises. The broad benefits offered by this book include learning of AI-based entrepreneurial modeling by synchronizing technology interface with enterprise planning using AI, ML, AR, VR, and IoT networking for entrepreneurial transitions. Improving skills on knowledge management, co-intelligence (AI-human interface), and collaborative approaches in entrepreneurial transformation.

It is import to restructure backward and forward infrastructure to adapt to AI and Cloud environment. Benefits of this book also extends in understanding AI-led production and services management in micro, small, and medium enterprises.

This book offers macro analysis by converging divergent factors on AI-led decision making to strengthen the competitive standing of micro, small, and medium enterprises. Simultaneously, the discussion in the book also provides a think tank to analyze through the decision-conflict-choices model to understand the behavioral dilemmas in adapting to the AI frameworks. The organization of thematic sections across chapters adheres to logical flow of ideas, thematic linearity, interconnectivity of learning nodes, and channelizing best practices and case studies through the thematic discussions in the book. Each chapter has an overview at the beginning, which helps in appraising the following discussions in the chapter while main points of discussion in the chapter is summarized at the end. Accordingly, this book culminates into a new and comprehensive learning tool and a valuable guide for students and working managers in the areas of relevance.

Thematic Flow

This book is divided into five chapters across three parts comprising technology and human factors, AI and entrepreneurship, and navigation ahead respectively. Thematically, discussions on Growth in Technology (Chap. 2) and Technology and Human Factors (Chap. 3) are included in Part I while AI at Grassroots (Chap. 4) and Business Modeling (Chap. 5) are included in Part II of the book. Discussion with focus on future perspectives of navigation across cyberspace has been discussed in Chap. 6 in Part III of the book.

Technology has evolved across a series of stages from early tools and amateur machines to modern automations and digital revolutions. The growth of technology is faster than the growth in technology adaptation. New technologies such as Artificial Intelligence (AI) and machine learning significantly contribute to improving designing and production processes and form the basis for many new products with comparatively high levels of value-added.[15] Chapter 2 discusses chronological growth in technology harnessing diverse perspectives of the role of technology in the entrepreneurship 5.0 and advances in social development. Advances in technology has also driven co-intelligence, a concept with two distinct meanings-one focusing on the partnership between human and AI.[16] Contextual to various perspectives of technology, this chapter discusses managing co-intelligence in the knowledge-intensive enterprises. The core discussions are supported by the two brief case studies on Commonwealth Bank and AI in Chinese Food Business, in this chapter.

Socio-technical systems have been increasingly reliant on digital technologies to the point of some of them being more accurately described as cyber-socio-technical systems. Technological advances and outbreak of AI

[15] Broekel, T. & Klarl, T. (2025). The long-term evolution of technological complexity and its relationship with economic growth. *Technovation*, 144 (in press) https://doi.org/10.1016/j.technovation.2025.103233

[16] Mollick, E. (2025). *Co-intelligence-Living and Working with AI.* New York: Penguin Random House.

engagement have exhibited promising platforms for transforming various aspects of human life including education, entertainment, healthcare, manufacturing, customer services, and sustainability. In view of technology-human convergence, Chap. 3 discusses various perspectives of AI and cognitive ergonomics that affect entrepreneurial mind-set and systems thinking. Systems thinking in entrepreneurship encourages continuous learning and skill development to match with changing preferences of consumers and market competition. Applying systems thinking within the social and stakeholder ecosystem offers applied learning to firms, which enables them to enhance social proximity and systematically break the chaotic information to synthesize crowd-based business model.[17] Discussions also envelop the scope and outcome of technology empowerment among micro, small, and medium enterprises and arguments on disruptive technologies that affect entrepreneurial competitiveness. Case study on Cobalt Robotics, replacing workplace humans supplement the core discussions in the chapter on technology and human factors.

Contextualizing entrepreneurship with AI and changing business scenarios Chap. 4 focuses on narrowing the technological proximity of enterprises to simplify decision-making process. In this context, the fifth wave symbolizing the growth of AI and ML as revolutionary technology agents has been addressed in the chapter. The extensive application of AI and ML in data analytics, deep learning, and business modeling have been critically examined in this chapter by explaining the role of AI and ML in real-time decision making and gaining immersive experience in business modeling. Discussion on advances in digital technologies, which have increased the possibilities of open innovation and outsourcing entrepreneurial activities to explore new opportunities, have also added value to this chapter.[18] The case studies on McCormic & company and Champo Carpets of India provide applied insights on the use of AI in business modeling and operations, which broadly supports the salient features on AI discussed in this chapter.

AI-based business modeling offers a framework that integrates AI into core business functions to create, deliver, and capture value to leverage automated tasks and data-driven decision making. The potential

[17] A. Tittel, O. Terzidis (2020), Entrepreneurial competences revised: Developing a consolidated and categorized list of entrepreneurial competences. Entrepreneurship Education, 3(1), 1–35.

[18] Täuscher, K. (2017). Leveraging collective intelligence: How to design and manage crowd-based business models. *Business Horizons*, 60(2), 237–245.

application of AI in business processes is broad. Data-driven decision making using real-time AI tools optimizes decision-making procedures and amplifies their accuracy and reliability.[19] Chapter 5 on business modeling addresses AI infrastructure planning, AI-based designing and manufacturing, supply chain management, and semantic methods for business processes explaining the role of AI. The case study on HubSpot and Motion AI endorses the discussion of business modeling using AI in the chapter.

Chapter 6 addresses potential innovation in existing technologies driving AI and ML beyond business and sectoral applications. Technology shift specifically addresses the next generation AI to serve the generative and predictive AI to manage complex scenarios of AI-human interface in the cyberspace ahead. The next generation AI and ML leads to entrepreneurial transformation, which contributes to critical success of the firm from the perspective of strategic competitive success. NLP-related applications such as DeepSeek and ChatGPT, which have become popular recently are growing with hierarchical relationships between the concepts of AI, ML, and deep learning (DL). Deep learning models are practical for end-to-end learning pipelines because they can automatically extract features and have high future potential in combination with ML.[20] The changing role of AI in sectoral development in the context of healthcare, agriculture, and sustainability has been discussed in this chapter. Besides the future prospects of AI and ML in changing decision making, and business and sectoral development the role of AI in social technology that affect the future geo-economic and business scenarios have also been deliberated in this chapter with focus on transformational AI and entrepreneurship. Discussions also emphasize the role of government in supporting entrepreneurial transformation by resolving the visible and invisible challenges embedded in local firms.[21] Drawing the synergy from

[19] Battisti, S., Agarwal, N., & Brem, A. (2022). Creating new tech entrepreneurs with digital platforms: Meta-organizations for shared value in data-driven retail ecosystems. *Technological Forecasting and Social Change*, 175 (2), in press. https://doi.org/10.1016/j.techfore.2021.121392

[20] Golec, M., Hatay, E. S., Gill, S. S., & Buyya, R. (2025). Artificial Intelligence (AI): Foundations, trends and future directions. *Telematics and Informatics Reports*, 20, in press https://doi.org/10.1016/j.teler.2025.100265.

[21] Liu, S. C.-H. and Lee, T. (2019). The multilevel effects of transformational leadership on entrepreneurial orientation and service innovation. *International Journal of Hospitality Management*, 82, 278–286.

the previous chapters, a synthesis on entrepreneurial transformation has been discussed in Chap. 6 by convergence of divergent transformational factors and the philosophy of knowing-doing-being.

Fit Within the Learning Ecosystem

Anyone who intends to be a potential entrepreneur using contemporary technology deserves learning resources in an evidenced-based entrepreneurial business modeling that engages with advanced technologies in entrepreneurship to experience the changing philosophy of knowing-doing-being. This book helps readers to explore new concepts like the synergy between AI and human factors, AI-led business modeling, and working with the real-time business ecosystem. The discussion in this book synchronizes technology framework, sensitivity analysis (probabilities of cost, time, and risk factors), and many such concepts that are less explained but more practiced. This book fills the existing learning resources gap by converging AI-based entrepreneurship with the best practices, success, and failure case studies by integrating the logically connect in decision making. This book complements to the existing books on entrepreneurial technology and competitive growth as discussed above. The principal audience of this book are potential researchers interested in conducting research based on entrepreneurial practices and their contributions to organizational design and operational efficiency in sustainable enterprises. This book helps to establish new research dimensions on convergence of entrepreneurial practices and dimensions of organizational development in emerging markets. This book also serves as a reference for the students of graduate management program studying in entrepreneurship stream, for learning the green entrepreneurial management patterns in emerging markets as suggested under Sustainable Development Goals.

We hope this book will contribute to the existing literature and deliver new concepts to the students and researchers to pursue the subject further. By reading this book, policy makers, non-governmental organizations, and entrepreneurship development agencies will develop insights on how to converge innovation, technology, and business practices under changing entrepreneurial conditions.

October 30, 2025, Mexico City

PART I

Technology and Human Factors

CHAPTER 2

Growth in Technology

The Chronological Growth

Technological evolution, which describes adaptation and evolution behavior among species in accordance with the changing needs, can be analogically explained in the context of the principles of evolutionary biology. Therefore, technological evolution is symbiotic to human needs driven by innovation, adaptation, selection, and continuous refinement over the existing conditions for survival and sustainability (Laland et al., 2015). New ideas and invention are the initial stages to redesign the existing knowledge, where technology plays a significant role in modifying and refining the existing processes to better fit specific human needs in socio-economic context. Social and industrial technologies are interdependent for economic development to meet dynamic challenges to reshape living, working, and interacting within the global geodemographic space. The continuous growth in commoditization and commercialization process has stimulated the evolution of technology over time to enable economic growth in a streamlined pattern. Consequently, innovation has grown as a technology derivative to streamline the changing needs of people, market, supply chain, manufacturing, entrepreneurship, and services. However, disruptive innovations have always been ahead of strategic, social, and commercial innovations, which focus more on tactical output causing

Rajagopal, A. Rajagopal, *Artificial Intelligence and Entrepreneurship*, Palgrave Studies of Entrepreneurship and Social Challenges in Developing Economies,
https://doi.org/10.1007/978-3-032-14904-6_2

off-track impacts. Over time, technological growth has been linked to the market lifecycle, which attracts new technology, radical entrepreneurs, and global visionaries (Moore, 2004).

Evolution of technology is a continuous process, which is independent of political, economic, and social intervening factors. Technology has evolved across series of stages from early tools and amateur machines to modern automations and digital revolutions. The growth of technology is faster than the growth in technology adaptation. The diffusion of technology largely depends on knowledge management, its application to social, economic, and industrial development, and capabilities and competencies among the users to manage transformation synchronizing with social and economic requirements. With the advancement of technology education and use value perceived by people, modern society including enterprises and entrepreneurs have become more dependent on information and technology, and the benefits embedded in deploying quality in manufacturing, marketing, operations, and entrepreneurial sectors. However, the major concern toward adaptation to technology largely depends on its economic viability, cost-time-risk (CRT) associations, technology lifecycle, and its feasibility in various business functions. It has been observed that the rapid growth of technology has shortened the technology lifecycle because of rapid shifts in generations, quicker end-of-life phenomenon, and changes in operational platforms. Consequently, the concept of *technological waves* has attracted technocrats, entrepreneurs, decision-makers, and business leaders to improve continuously the technology impact on production, operations, sustainability, sectorial development, and natural ecosystems. Technology has been significantly adopted in developing Industry, Innovation, and Infrastructure (I-3 factors) to achieve responsible consumption and production. The Sustainable Development Goals and public governance in developed and developing countries have encouraged technology transitions to improve public economy and renascence of industries with continuous evolution of technology for cleaner production, consumption, and entrepreneurship (Almgren & Skobelev, 2020).

Continuous evolution of information and communication technologies (ICT) has significantly driven digitalization of conventional business processes and the concept of Internet of Things (IOT) in business. The competitive engagement of firms with virtual technologies tends to unveil new entrepreneurial models (EMs) within hybrid environments. This phenomenon has extensively contributed to the continuous growth of the new business economy in a hybrid environment. Such business impetus is developed around the so-called metaverses. In the cyber-physical ecosystem, EMs have been developed as a combination of physical- and virtual-world mechanisms that help in developing social and economic values. Reviewing the changing technological perspectives, Artificial Intelligence (AI) is often considered the 'fifth wave' of computing aided by machine learning (ML), which contributes to major transformative technological advancement that is currently shaping various industries and aspects of life, characterized by autonomous AI systems capable of operating independently in complex environments (Kim, 2024). Economic creation and value capture, at the crossroads of physical and virtual economies today, are enabled through the cyber revolution comprising AI, AR, VR, and metaverse. Digital technology, which has shown significant positive effect on quality function deployments in manufacturing, marketing, and operations, has emerged as an outgrowth of information and communication technologies. The digital platforms support innovation, entrepreneurship, and development nexus, which manifests in social and economic growth. The digital technology innovation has emerged as the fifth wave of industrial transformation by creating mixed effects on innovation-driven growth, entrepreneurial spirit, and automation strategy. Consequently, the growth in technology has exhibited both challenges and opportunities in adopting new technologies by making transitions at grassroots in revamping the EMs, strategies, and economic re-structures. The digital capabilities of entrepreneurs have been significantly supported by the governments in developing countries. Consequently, the technology transitions at grassroots enterprises are central to innovation, quality-growth, and performance. The digital transformations extend beyond adopting new technologies and are increasingly central to market competitiveness, which gives impetus to entrepreneurs to improve economic resources, sustainable practices, and stay out-of-the-box to overcome conventional wisdom and remain critical to market competition and capitalize on the use of technology (Ma et al., 2025).

Entrepreneurship 5.0

Technological advancement and continuous innovation have emerged as a fundamental source of economic growth and revolutionized entrepreneurship beyond conventional wisdom. The new technologies in various sectors of economic and sociological development have established new processes with value additions to improve the overall trio of humanization, industrialization, and commercialization. It is a cumulative and combinative process which stimulates innovation to build new ideas on existing knowledge and develop recombination of advanced technologies, capabilities, and competencies. The homogeneity and heterogeneity of technological capabilities are derived through geo-economic and geo-political needs and philosophies respectively (Šmihula, 2010). In recent years, technological growth and adaptability have shifted to new complexities due to the geo-factors as discussed above with focus on Power, Economy, and Governance (PEG). However, the bottom-line of technological evolution is to cater to the changing needs and determine strategic Sustainability, Survival, and social development (S-3 factors). The economic complexities across geo-commercial and geo-demographic global span require sophisticated technology and knowledge refinement to exhibit positive relationship between the PEG and S-3 factors.

Despite allocating enormous resources across developed and emerging economies, technological growth has not been homogeneous as emerging economies at the bottom-of-the-pyramid are not yet adapted to technological innovations. It requires strengthening the enterprises economically at the grassroots by providing adequate financial resources and improving risk taking abilities to adapt to new technologies and match with the global speed and magnitude of technology-led industrial progress. One of the key enablers to technology adaptation is General Purpose Technologies (GPT) aiming at improving conventional wisdom and developing intentions to innovate through technological drivers (Evangelista et al., 2018).

Evolution of technology is a continuous process, which is impacting global, social, and economic development. Though the growth of technology is independent, it is founded on the pyramidal constituents of market, economy, and society as exhibited in Fig. 2.1. The changing trends in market have driven the technology growth manifold to match with the industrial, societal, and consumption needs by innovating affordable new products. Technology-based business modeling has restructured the market operations including logistics, supply chain, retailing, and consumerism. Digitization, as a principal factor of technology evolution, is fundamentally changing the market modeling approaches through automated information systems, analytical techniques, and strategic approaches in micro, small, and medium enterprises at the grassroots. The availability of digital data combined with market-oriented technology platforms has significantly supported the digital business modeling process to impact the

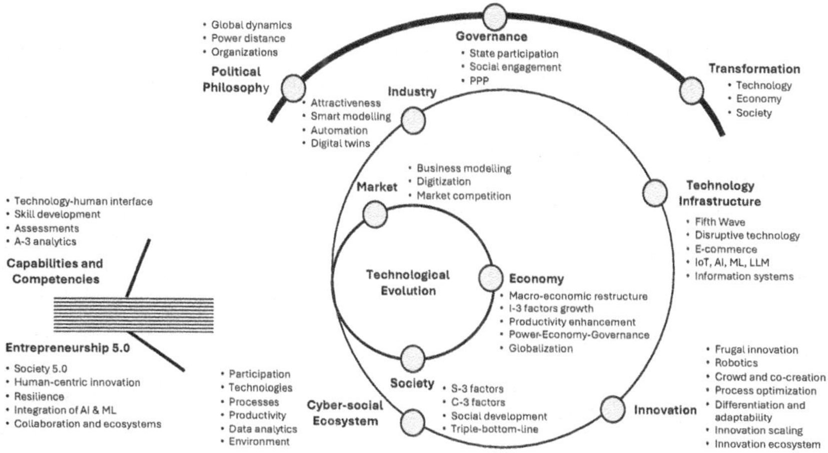

Fig. 2.1 Technology evolutions ecosystems. (Source: Authors)

traceable market operations to improve efficiency. The use of AI and ML enables enterprises to identify new work processes, production, and logistics patterns to optimize marketing performance and predict consumer behavior. The new trend in business modeling is growing rapidly by using simulations with the help of digital agents to map market dynamics and match the challenges of personalized marketing, omni channel marketing, and dynamic pricing. Consequently, the growth in information and communication technology has driven new analytical techniques, which are significantly affecting the young enterprises (start-ups) in adapting to *go-to-market* strategy. However, the advancement of marketing technologies has scaled up the market competition by enhancing continuously the customer value and providing confidence in decision making using AI-customer interfaces on user-friendly technology platforms.

Technology development and its adoption in enterprises widely depend on macro-economic factors including resource allocation, productivity, innovation, and contribution to economic growth. The resources for developing and managing technology have a wide range of options comprising government funding, corporate investments, foreign direct investments, and individual capital allocations at various levels of technology development and diffusion. Governments in developing economies have come up with several funding initiatives to support technology as a governance system through regulatory measures, which provides agencies with funding to modernize IT systems, process platforms, and improve the existing IT infrastructure to enhance end-user delivery systems. The funding programs in developing economies encourage technology-based productivity target of start-up enterprises and minority entrepreneurship, which intends to support broadband IT infrastructure program to optimize Internet-of-Things (IoT) penetration. In addition, corporate investments in funding encourage companies to allocate funds for IT projects, infrastructure upgrades, and procurement of software licenses. This approach enables IT growth in diverse sectors to improve productivity and attract venture capitalists to further invest in emerging technology companies. In financial markets, private equity firms (PEFs) invest in high-performance companies to improve technology operations and restructure the aging technologies. PEFs also acquire budding technologies created by start-up enterprises and intend to commercialize such technology platforms for enhanced adoptability to support diverse operations to improve productivity as illustrated in Fig. 2.1. Large enterprises set up corporate ventures to invest in technology-driven start-up firms to foster frugal innovation and encourage technology use across the industry and society. In addition, crowdfunding has emerged as a new option to fund technology initiatives at the grassroots. Platforms like Kickstarter and Indiegogo allow individual entrepreneurs to solicit funds for new ideas, donations, or start-up business. Fintech institutions enable amateur entrepreneurs to invest in diverse business ideas, raise business differentiators, and develop technology platforms and applications for use in industry and society. However, the major challenge in technology funding is to determine the technology lifecycle, cost-benefit ratio, and risk factors as the growth of technology across various sectors is faster than the rate of diffusion and adoption.

Developing nascent enterprises in incubators is one of the major economic and technological challenges, which requires macro-economic policy support on I-3 factors comprising industry development aligned with technology growth (industry 5.0), frugal innovation (low-cost adaptable innovations), and technology infrastructure (AI, ML, and e-commerce). These factors contribute significantly to technology venture creation on advanced collaborative workspaces like cloud environment, to resolve entrepreneurship-technology nexus. The proactive strategies for technology start-up incubators and the political philosophy driving micro-economic policies and economic governance significantly help in mitigating conflicts within entrepreneurship-technology nexus (van Erkelens et al.,

2024). Besides economic factors, entrepreneurship-technology convergence is widely supported by societal factors comprising social development, sustainability, and social digitization (S-3 factors). Social development and sustainability are symbiotic and broadly conform to Sustainable Development Goals. The technological development addressing social PNS factors has higher proximity and outreach with increased possibilities of adaptation to technology-led environments. Social technologies are broadly referred to sustainable stewardship in the sectors of energy, transportation, agriculture, industry, and seamless education. Accordingly, the triple-bottom-line postulation comprising People, Planet, and Profit lead to benefit the people-oriented technology with social concerns.

Besides core (market, economy, and society) and peripheral (industry, technology, infrastructure, innovation, and cyber-social ecosystem) factors associated with technological innovation, the political philosophy on internet usage and cyber governance significantly affect the technology transformation to nascent enterprises in developing economies. Political factors stimulate organizational empowerment on AI to cope up with global dynamics and geo-political and geo-business power distance as exhibited in Fig. 2.1. The cyber governance is a framework of policies, processes, and practices, which are designed, developed, and implemented to ensure ethical development and application of generative and predictive AI (Holmström & Hällgren, 2022). The major concern in regulating AI development and application is to marginalize the risks, biasness, and misuse of AI information in disrupting business and socio-psychological behavior of entrepreneurs and stakeholders. Governments in most developing economies are engaged in establishing ethical standards of AI governance ensuring alignment of AI with human values to promote social and business well-being within the framework of industrial standards and growth perspectives. One of the major challenges in developing and using AI is synchronizing the processes and inculcating accountability to deploy AI governance aligning with safety, security, and ethical standards. Promoting entrepreneurial confidence in responsible innovation, business development, and social upliftment requires trust building by lowering the risk factors such as biases, security and privacy breaches (Meske et al., 2022). Therefore, fostering public-private collaboration between stakeholders, developers, business leaders, and policy makers is a major challenge in achieving such synchronization. AI governance needs to focus on protecting human rights, dignity, and fundamental freedom by ensuring accountability, social values, and trust as key perspectives in balancing innovation and business growth. International organizations like UNESCO and OECD are engaged in developing the framework of AI policy and ethical norms to promote international cyber regulations and technology-led industrial initiatives. Consequently, the AI governance is a dynamic and continuously evolving field, which requires public, private, and state collaborations to address the NOISE elements comprising social and business *needs*, competitive *opportunities*, affordable *innovation*, business and technology *strengths*, and economic growth *expectations*. The responsible AI governance helps in differentiating the liberal technological growth and governance of AI in a socially responsible way (Papagiannidis et al., 2025). The convergence of political views on AI governance with technology transformation enables the growth in economy, entrepreneurship, and society.

Entrepreneurship 5.0 is in practice, a representation of technology-based entrepreneurial landscape founded on Industry 5.0 (AI and robotics) and Society 5.0 (digital network and communication). It synchronizes with ambidextrous growth of industry and business with the reinforcement of human-centric innovation by leveraging advanced technologies like AI and data analytics to create solutions for societal needs and promote sustainability. Human centricity in Entrepreneurship 5.0 prioritizes human needs and well-being to address innovation, which supports the PNS factors by integrating AI, IoT, and data analytics. The use of AI and ML in entrepreneurial processes such as design, development, and delivery enable agility and real-time adaptability to match with the changing market conditions and stay competitive. Entrepreneurship 5.0 demonstrates human-centric innovations, resilience, public-private collaboration, and alignment with changing social and business ecosystems by improving capabilities and competencies and A-3 analytics comprising ambitions alignments, and actions to improve technology-human interface.

The fifth wave of technological evolution supported by AI, ML, and large language modeling (LLM) has led to support industrial development through information management, data analytics, and predictive modeling in manufacturing and services. Smart technology modeling embeds wide range of approaches from conceptual models to simulation modeling using logarithmic mapping of variables for decision making. The conceptual technological modeling for micro, small, and medium enterprises represents smart systems with sensors and seamless operations, data-based decision matrix, and point-to-point interactions to improve manufacturing and services systems. Smart technologies facilitate communication and help in developing business-process modeling for emerging firms using data analytics and data visualization leading to simulations enabling entrepreneurs to monitor dynamic production, logistics, and marketing operations (Giliyana et al., 2025). The *Digital Twins* are virtual representation of physical assets in complex processes linked with simulations to optimize manufacturing, logistics, and other business operations in various industrial sectors (Mihai et al., 2022). The industry 5.0 converges the smart technology and business modeling through strategic alignment, process optimization, innovation, adaptability and efficiency, and sustainability to create unique value propositions for the end users.

The contemporary stage of technology evolution, which is referred to as fifth wave, requires significant investment in technological infrastructure to support processes, e-commerce, and technology modeling for manufacturing and services. The new stage of industrial revolution combines human skills with Artificial Intelligence (AI) and machine learning (ML) to improve the efficiency and accuracy of mechanical output controlled by robotics. Emerging enterprises of various sizes across the cyber-physical space in the global ecosystem are relying on AI and ML by improving human abilities in computer-aided creativity, decision-making, and solving complex problems. The industry 5.0 accordingly sets a new trend in business by encouraging highly personalized and demand-led manufacturing through AI and ML advantages (Huang et al., 2022). The growing new markets have shown high industry attractiveness with increase in market competition and simultaneous substitution effects in manufacturing, marketing, and consumption of products and services. The economic shifts and social changes contributed to enhancing the bargaining power of consumers and suppliers, which aggravated market disruptions including fragmentation of markets. These technologies converge collaborative robotics, exoskeleton, and augmented reality (AR) within sophisticated AI systems. The emerging firms today use virtual reality (VR), augmented reality, and metaverse reality (MR) to establish closer interaction between human elements and machine-led business. It is the right time for firms to evaluate the threats and opportunities in the technology transitions and create appropriate business models to connect with advanced digital ecosystem (Xu et al., 2021). Service enterprises like Airbnb, Uber, and Amazon are gradually driving transition of their services to leverage customer relationships and reduce the cost-time-risk (CTR) factors. The major challenge in such transition process is to integrate value chains of conventional systems with the new technology ecosystem and develop distinctive business models by enhancing capabilities, competencies, and business relationships.

Transcending technology and innovations have significantly penetrated new order of entrepreneurship with emphasis on AI and automation, which is referred as *Entrepreneurship in Society 5.0*. The new paradigm in entrepreneurship with the integration of technology has developed human interfaces to generate value to drive innovation and sustainable growth (Appio et al., 2021). Entrepreneurship 5.0 has revolutionized the role of technology to develop societal challenges by integrating human ingenuity. Consequently, economic progress and societal well-being are seen as an outgrowth of technology-driven entrepreneurship by not undermining the importance of human-centered approach to address PNS factors, values, and advancements in knowledge. The technological revolution in the entrepreneurship at the grassroots encompasses Sustainable Development Goals (SDGs) to promote long-term societal well-being by considering the triple bottom-line. The automation practices in entrepreneurship leverage digital technologies and AI to develop advanced solutions to designing, manufacturing, operations, and services. The adaptation to AI-based technological platforms has brought agility in entrepreneurial activities enabling entrepreneurs to develop synchronization with changing market conditions and consumer preferences. The new Entrepreneurship 5.0 is evolving around collaborations and networking among the industry players, bottom-line entrepreneurs, technology experts, and stakeholders to facilitate problem solving and experience sharing to endorse the shifts in knowledge. Accordingly, the technological revolution in entrepreneurship leverages creativity, productivity, and market competitiveness with sustainable, equitable, and future prosperity (Çipi et al., 2023).

Digital transformation has significantly driven the practices of entrepreneurship 5.0 and stimulated changes in design thinking, manufacturing, marketing operations and business communications at multiple levels. Digitization and automation of entrepreneurial activities have contributed to innovating new opportunities by sensing complex business situations and resizing the scale of business to harness competitive advantages despite disruptive effects and conventional wisdom of entrepreneurs. Broadly, the concept of Society 5.0 can be explained as a smart society with the growing human society interface to cater to variety of needs and narrowing down the gaps in value and lifestyle and other social domains such as health, education, agriculture, supply chain, logistics, and disaster management (Huang et al., 2022). Society 5.0 initiatives also address institutional and individual reforms to enable the adoption of technology-led business models and technology education to promote innovation as a pathway to new order globalization. However, Entrepreneurship 5.0 and Society 5.0 need to balance the relationship between Technology, Entrepreneurs, and Society (TES) to explore collaborative socio-economic opportunities. Therefore, the TES factors need to be coordinated on both cyber-space and physical space converging cognitive advancements and applied information of the real time. Technology for business and society must develop new combinations to rope in society and entrepreneurship over the conventional models that already exist. Accordingly, society can focus on improving enterprises at the grassroots by encouraging digitization and restructuring new values to improve productivity and business, while entrepreneurship may focus on adapting to new technologies to gain added value in entrepreneurial economics and social equity (Nagy & Hajrizi, 2019).

The advancement of information and communication technology, digitization, and technology-aided business models have attracted a large number of start-up enterprises with innovative ideas and applied platforms. Besides adapting technologies in the physical workspaces, technology-oriented entrepreneurs have also shown affiliation to emerging trend of metaverse, which is a collective, shared, and virtual space built by the convergence of cyber and physical reality. It is a shared virtual space with the integration of AR and VR deploying digital assets and Avatars by technology entrepreneurs. In addition, the technology-led enterprises (large or start-ups) are focusing on the ***digital-twins*** model representing the virtual manifestation of a physical object or a system updated in real-time data using sensors. Young enterprises are engaged in supporting large firms engaged in supply chain and logistics management with the ***digital-twins*** model for real time tracking of objects through data analysis, simulation, and monitoring physical movements to optimize geo-physical operations (Zhang et al., 2025).

Harnessing Diverse Perspectives

The new generation entrepreneurship is widely led by the adaptive technologies such as AI and ML emerging out of diverse social and economic perspectives. Technological entrepreneurship led to addressing innovation in diverse sectors providing inclusive solutions and mitigating social and technological biases to serve a broad range of human needs. The diverse perspectives of adaptive technologies include economics of innovation, scaling of technology, and risk factors by combining creative and innovative viewpoints to approach problem-solving exercises. In this process, diverse technological teams help entrepreneurial gaps across the above perspectives and contribute to development process by narrowing down the apparent and latent cognitive and technological biases. Adapting to technology-led new generation entrepreneurship, social inclusivity needs to be ensured by involving people from diverse socio-economic backgrounds and entrepreneurial potential to develop a social consensus on adaptability to AI- and ML-based technological platforms. Leveraging diverse teams across geo-demographic and geo-economic belts, entrepreneurship can be restructured by building technology skills and integrating entrepreneurial experiences to take efficient decisions on innovation and related techno-economic perspectives. The community forums of new generation entrepreneurs in developing economies emerge from diverse socio-economic and knowledge backgrounds, which are largely under supported by the global technology forums to collaborate latent demands on technology adaptation and innovation (Lee et al., 2025). Broadly, the diverse perspectives in the context of technology-led new generation entrepreneurship constitute the macro- and micro-economics of technology, frugal innovation, inclusivity in entrepreneurship and business, common workspace for collaborative adaptation to technology, ethical considerations, and mitigating social and individual biases.

The rapid growth in transformative technologies, broadly identify as extensive use of AI, cloud computing, and mobile devices has significantly encouraged technology-led enterprises at the grassroots. The user perception and acceptance of transformative technologies have identified a range of artificial design features to determine future oriented entrepreneurial models and knowledge-based collaborations from socio-technological and techno-economic perspectives. These features of future technology adaptation are revolutionizing the business processes by integrating data analytics, automation, and real-time insights to support continuous innovation and market dynamics. The enormous volume of data available on cloud platforms and sensors enable entrepreneurial AI projects to work on real time data and innovate products and processes to match with the desired PNS factors and market potential. This widespread transformative technology phenomenon has not only helped in developing and positioning market-based innovations but also stimulated human cognitive activities in reshaping entrepreneurial thinking by transforming the conventional knowledge and nature of work. Expert systems are successfully associating with the process of AI adaptation to entrepreneurship backed by machine learning and immersive experience. Linking new opportunities to AI-based entrepreneurial designs and cognitive decision-making platforms, neural entrepreneurial networks are growing rapidly across various economic sectors. However, the complexity in human-computer interface in developing economies tend to marginalize the effects of technology-led new generation entrepreneurship and transforming entrepreneurial structures to meet the dynamic social and economic challenges (Wang et al., 2024). Therefore, the socio-technological perspectives need to be analyzed in the context of adapting to technology at the initial stage of entrepreneurial transformation.

One of the complex factors in technology management is the economics of technology in the context of cost, breakeven, and risk related variables, which affects innovation and productivity in enterprises operating at various scales. Consequently, the choice of technology adoption is governed by enterprise economic factors that are critical to cost of technology, investment and lifecycle, and associated risks of technology failures. Innovations, operations, and production-oriented technologies can be adopted by enterprises of various scales of operation by validating the productivity gains and profit perspectives. The changing market structures due to dynamic competition significantly affect the economics of technology from the point-of-view of technology adoption to gain economic efficiency and market competitiveness. The cost of testing technologies and validation to apply them often takes long time, which includes also longitudinal perspectives of technology, which can be described as the upcoming technology generations. Consequently, delay in technology validation from the perspective of its feasibility and economic viability discourages adaptation process in enterprises. As the growth of technology is independent to the economic variables, the delay in validation of technology and its adaptability does not prevent the generation growth of technologies. In this context, the new generations of technology quickly drive the current technologies obsolete. Therefore, despite opportunities in adoption of new technologies, there is a delay in adaptation process at enterprise level due to risk factors, cost implications, and technology yield patterns. However, AI-based technology and innovation emerge as a vital pathway in transforming entrepreneurial practices and embedded business models by optimizing productivity and enhancing business modeling (Kliestik et al., 2024).

To address the challenges of adopting innovating technologies and leveraging AI to enhance productivity and profitability, firms need to improve capabilities and competencies in technology applications and redesign process paradigms for successful deployment of AI and new technologies over the economic challenges. In this context, firms can manage the complexity in economics of technology by integrating knowledge-based view to focus the productivity of technology by adjusting the CTR factors to augment productivity and develop market competitiveness. The adaptive behavior of key partners in an enterprise (employees, consumers, and collaborative firms) largely serves as moderator in optimizing technology-based productivity and marginalizing the risk by connecting with applied market insights (Zu et al., 2025). The impact of AI-driven technological innovations varies by the type of industry, scale of business, ownership structure, and geographic location, which determines the extent of positive effects on productivity and profitability of entrepreneurial firms. However, it is important for the firms to analyze the CTR factors associated with transactional technologies such as blockchain management by applying the cost and revenue concepts to the economics of technology before adopting less known industrial technologies (Ahluwalia et al., 2020). Amidst economic challenges, AI technologies represent several entrepreneurship opportunities including real time business models and start-up financing using robust business approaches uncovering the embedded risks of technology adoption in enterprises (Tumasjan et al., 2019).

Design-to-market strategies over time have become a common practice as entrepreneurial marketing. The entrepreneurial marketing approach involves cost-effective activities by avoiding formal market research or involving mass promotions strategies to promote business (Moore & Manring, 2009). However, entrepreneurs of small and medium business segments significantly depend on their personal networks to collect information about consumers and the market. Therefore, managing an emerging enterprise requires adequate market research, strategy development skills, outsource key activities, and automation of operations. Start-up endeavors generally involve numerous activities performed by the entrepreneurs to attain resources and process them into innovative products or services to fill the previously identified gap between the market-offer and the consumer-needs. Therefore, these enterprises tend to engage in identifying opportunities and market advantages to fulfill the customer's needs. Competitive advantage is built by enterprises in an increasingly interconnected global economy. Entrepreneurial firms collaborating with local enterprises often innovate their business models. Firms tend to work with computer aided design and development systems to switch to digitization, main hybridity, and mobile business applications. These firms develop design-to-market and collaborative business models (with stakeholders) for implementation through a set of activities to transform existing businesses based on a socio-economic model. A micro, small, or medium firm having a new idea, if expensive to produce commercially and either too early or too late to hit a market with weak brick-and-mortar operations, struggles to procure financing. Design thinking at the entrepreneurial level needs to fetch a great leap to develop compatibility with computer-aided designing embedding ethnic and crowd-based values. The synchronization of innovation and technology factors at the local level might have the potential to generate butterfly effect, which will attract reverse innovation and commercialization of entrepreneurial products in a wider market (Rajagopal, 2024).

Managing Co-intelligence

Collaborative relationship between humans and AI to achieve common goals can be referred to as co-intelligence, which involves critical thinking, innovation, and synchronizing human expectation by integrating AI metaknowledge to strengthen the A-3 factors. Intervention of AI enables breaking the stereotype and conventional wisdom with dogmatic effects among entrepreneurs and encourages to enhance human intelligence and creativity through systematic processing of information, causes, and effects. The contemporary practice in working with AI has been recognized as enabling a co-worker to partner in problem solving and creative endeavors. However, AI is not recommended as a replacement for humans but to stay with humans in the loop of knowledge management and technological transformation. AI-driven processes complement to PNS factors of the society and help in reducing human oversight and judgmental biasness provided AI is ethically, effectively, and efficiently used in entrepreneurial projects. Bringing AI to the workspace delimits traditional boundaries and prompts learning real-time craft effectiveness to achieve desired outputs, refine them digitally, and improve the outcomes treating AI as a partner. However, anthropomorphizing AI agents within logical frameworks can lead to better engagement of AI agents as entrepreneurial partners and activate human-computer interface with specific objectives. It is important to identify complex tasks where AI can enhance human capabilities by generating competitive ideas, analyzing data, and automating the repetitive and flagship tasks.

Working with an AI agent as a workspace assistant, entrepreneurs need to logically analyze the agreements and disagreements on AI-based suggestive information, designs, and deliverables by evaluating internal capabilities and competencies. However, an AI agent can help in mapping the business ecosystem and associated externalities to help decision making on entrepreneurial approaches within the supportive framework of human-computer interface. AI agent needs to be subjected to ethical considerations by eliminating the existing redundancies and biases while AI automates the tasks by fragmenting challenges and adapting approaches to co-intelligence. Embracing co-intelligence, entrepreneurs and organizations can harness the power of AI to innovate competitively and achieve market leadership over time. However, the anthropomorphism of AI often overrides human intelligence and stay sentient in entrepreneurial and social development processes. The co-intelligence is often recognized as a hybrid ecosystem supporting decision making and automation at a macro scale. The engagement of AI agents in entrepreneurship results in collaborative action, superior outcome, and continuous learning with flexibility, creativity, process emphasis, and business instinct.

Human-AI interaction can be recognized as hybrid intelligence, which involves goal-oriented approach with focus on collaborating natural and mechanical intelligence with complexities of ethical derivations and solution excellence. The SWOT (strength, weakness, opportunity, and threat) and VIRO (value, intelligence, rarity, and organization) analysis pursue better decision making on real time problems and predictions by contemplating the human-machine collaboration. Accordingly, collaborative, adaptive, and explainable AI engagement in entrepreneurship requires an ethics-oriented approach across four meta-dimensions comprising task attributes, learning paradigm, co-intelligence, and human emotions. These meta-dimensions help in analyzing the PNS factors of society and consumers as a part of hybrid intelligence system, which serves as an AI-human complimentary team. Consequently, the augmented intelligence emphasizes the concept of human-computer loop essential for purpose-oriented design and user-friendly product development. Figure 2.2 exhibits the human-computer loop in AI environment with embedded attributes and expectations.

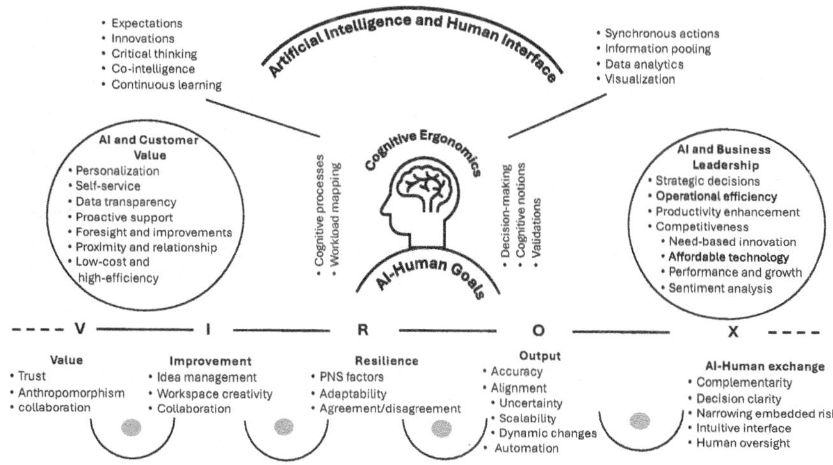

Fig. 2.2 Attributes of human-computer loop in AI environment. (Source: Authors)

Human-AI interface moderates decision making using pool information from cyberspace and exhibits analysis through various modalities comprising text, voice, and visual interfaces to create seamless and intuitive experience as illustrated in Fig. 2.2. The AI system tends to understand the complexity of a given business situation and develop creative output with options of possible solutions the effective collaboration between human and AI needs deep understanding of AI and ML limitations, convergence of mental models, and demonstrating transparency to enable AI in suggesting possible options for entrepreneurial decisions. The multi-model interactions on AI platforms enable entrepreneurs to move beyond text-based interactions and leverage voice, gesture, gaze, and other modalities to develop a blend of mechanical and intuitive-cognitive experiences. Designing AI interfaces with human-centered approach should aim at creating intuitive, efficient, and situational decisions to foster positive outcomes.

Cognitive ergonomics, which is an assimilation of tangible and intangible human factors connecting to multiple mental processes, is a complex set of human brains. It is challenging to develop accurate interface of human cognition with AI system, which leads to mixed experiences of agreements and disagreements on AI suggested outcomes. However, aligning human cognition with AI system helps in reducing cognitive workload, minimizing errors, and largely enhancing usability. The overload of cognitive processes leads to fatigue and human errors, which can be prevented by AI interactions to streamline the decision making through accuracy and information processing. Human cognition has often suffered with pre-conceived notions such as repetitive processes, embedded biases, and anticipated outcomes. The stereotype cognitive processes generate identical or marginally varied expectations, which require critical thinking and continuous learning to clean up the cognitive ergonomics and reinforce innovative thinking through co-intelligence (AI-Human interface) to achieve efficiency in decision making. The AI delimits cognitive horizon and provides synchronous (real time) actions through rigorous data analytics and visualization.

The AI-human goals are represented by VIROX factors in Fig. 2.2. It is a combination of intangible and tangible factors consisting of value, improvement, resilience, output, and AI-human exchange. The value perspectives constitute intangible elements like trust and anthropomorphism during the human-AI interface. To gain trust in AI system, the attribution of human traits, emotions, and intentions develop anthropomorphic orientation to perceive AI as collaborator in decision making. However, misinterpretations of AI decision options often complicate the adaptability and collaboration with AI-based platforms among entrepreneurs. Such misinterpretations are concerned with the capabilities and limitations of AI as human expectations often rise high on the ability of AI toward understanding complex situations and nuanced judgments. One of the common goals of human-AI interface is the perceived improvements in workspace creativity through effective ideas management and competitiveness. The resilience in AI-human interaction broadly refers to the embedded abilities and convergence of AI systems with users to adapt functionalities of machine learning and accept disruptions in the social and personal well-being. The robustness of AI system over the human ability to navigate complex information and decision interfaces describes the resilience in using the AI systems. In this process, the robustness of information analytics, adaptability, error management, transparency, and clarity in decision support constitutes the AI resilience (Teo, 2025). Entrepreneurial resilience in AI interactions is broadly knitted with cognitive and emotional capabilities, trust and reliance, social well-being, decision competencies, and judgments on fixing human errors. In human-AI interactions, the degree of complexity, fairness, and embedded goals can be explained in analyzing the PNS factors and enhancing the extent of adaptability on AI-based options overruling the peripheral disagreements (Tabibnia & Radecki, 2018).

AI output in entrepreneurship refers to accuracy in data analytics and interpretation of results to support decision making to align with probable risk factors, scalability of business, and market dynamics. It helps in various ways to leverage entrepreneurial decision making and enhance business operations by improving synchronous decision making. AI tools enable automation of tasks, leading to improved efficiency in scheduling tasks, streamlining workflows, handling customer service, and generating competitive advantage. AI-human exchange serves as complementarity in entrepreneurial decision making enabling intuitive interface and reducing redundancies in data points to narrow the risk factors. In addition, AI and entrepreneurial interfaces have significantly helped in reducing human oversight in making critical decisions. The role of AI in enhancing customer value and fostering business leadership is illustrated in Fig. 2.2, which argues that AI has emerged as an important tool in improving long-term decisions, operational efficiencies, productivity, and competitiveness through need-based innovations, affordable technology, and sentiment analysis to understand various perspectives of value chain. Customer value can be significantly enhanced through AI intervention in personalization, self-service initiatives, proactive support, proximity, and efficiency can be helpful in improving customer value.

Knowledge-Intensive Enterprises

Prioritizing knowledge **c**reation, **a**cquisition, **d**iffusion, and **a**pplication (CADA) are central to knowledge-intensive enterprises (KIEs), which rely heavily on AI-human interface. The growing digital micro-enterprises are largely based on knowledge-intensive tasks by using their experience, skills, and intellectual capital to create value, innovate, and drive economic growth in the competitive marketplace. These micro enterprises are largely run by amateurs who intend to invest in AI and cloud resources to focus on knowledge creation and dissemination. These enterprises operate in specific sectors like developing technology platforms, life senses, and advanced manufacturing through significant intervention of AI and cloud resources. The knowledge-intensive enterprises are often identified as disruptive entities in creating advanced knowledge on new product development, processes, and developing innovative consumer products over the existing ones. These enterprises have high ambidextrous reliance on AI and human capital to drive innovation through intensive research and development to impact knowledge-based economy (Liu et al., 2022). The KIEs deal with uncertainties to exploit innovative opportunities by analyzing NOISE factors in the context of market intelligence, capabilities, and competencies. Broadly, knowledge-based enterprises focus on strategies toward sustainability using NECTAR factor interface wherein the factor of NECTAR comprises nature (entrepreneurial attributes), economy (social well-being), culture (behavioral perspectives), technology (low-cost and AI-driven), activities (adaptation and perceived use value), and regulations (transparency and ethical considerations).

KIEs tend to employ highly skilled professionals with orientation on continuous learning and development to think ahead of innovation in developing new and competitive products with processes attributed to low-cost, short-time, and low-risk besides optimizing returns on capital employed. These enterprises are research- and development-intensive, which significantly invest in AI-driven innovation and technology platforms to acquire new knowledge, and develop eco-friendly and utilitarian products. KIEs also rely on crowd-based information available on social media channels, which is analyzed from the perspective of absorbing collective knowledge from crowd sources after eliminating possible redundancies. A broad range of KIEs include technology firms, developing AI and ML solutions, bio-technology solutions, and customer services such as financial and legal. MitiMeth,[1] a Nigeria-based innovative social enterprise engaged in manufacturing handicrafts products out of natural fiber extracted from agricultural waste and aquatic weeds has emerged as a nascent knowledge-intensive enterprise. This firm has added value in handicrafts products by transforming the waste into well-designed furniture and sustainable home furnishings. In this enterprise, AI is increasingly impacting its core business model on empowering artisans and marketing handicrafts with competitive strategies (PWC, 2025). This initiative of transforming the environmental based into marketable product has more than 600 artisan members across 25 communities in Nigeria. The AI intervention in this knowledge-intensive enterprise has significantly contributed to design thinking, innovative product development, and developing competitive marketing strategies as a resource for social well-being. This is one of the contributing factors to the Nigerian economy with

[1] For details see https://tinyurl.com/MitiMeth

application of AI-based knowledge repositories and task automation to improve the conventional wisdom and empower the social mission of artisans in modernizing traditional crafts (Gulawani, 2022).

Co-intelligence in entrepreneurship converges on an AI-human interface to synchronize information input for making business decisions to achieve efficiency in output and stay competitive in the marketplace. Such synchronization largely relies on continuous knowledge demonstrating intensiveness in restructuring entrepreneurship to gain real-time market advantages as indicated in Fig. 2.3. The knowledge component in this process tends to acquire real-time information and manage appropriate diffusion of knowledge within enterprise to induce creativity with the support of technology platforms and applications. In KIEs, the intellectual value relies on the trust in AI agents and supply of information from various sources in cloud repositories. However, AI enables information quality filters to improve trust and reliance as behavioral factors and supports continuous learning. The intensiveness of co-intelligence in enterprises of various sizes contributes to economic growth and competitive advantage by integrating AI-human interface through various technology services. Consequently, the AI agents significantly drive co-intelligence among

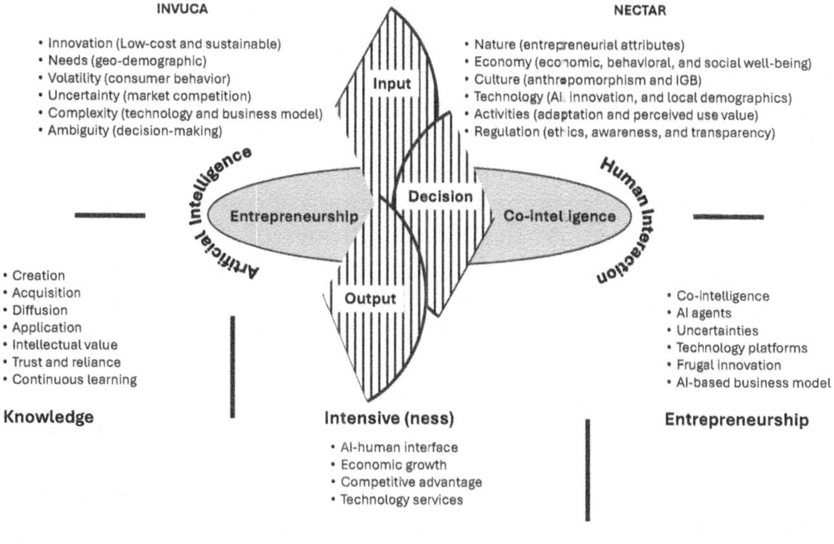

Fig. 2.3 Attributes of knowledge-intensive enterprises. (Source: Authors)

entrepreneurs through technology platforms to overcome predictable risks and unprecedented jeopardy in business. Broadly, entrepreneurs using AI agents find an in-depth think-tank to enable creative designs and processes in developing AI-driven entrepreneurial business models. While synchronizing input, decisions, and output process through co-intelligence, most entrepreneurs face the INVUCA challenge to develop low-cost and sustainable *innovation* to meet geo-demographic *needs* overriding the *volatility* in consumer behavior and fixing *uncertainties* emerging out of market competition managing technology and business model *complexities* through AI-guided decision making to overcome embedded *ambiguities*.

Adapting to Artificial Intelligence is sine qua non for knowledge-intensive enterprises, which heavily rely on co-intelligence skills converging human and AI interface to create value through continuous innovation and business growth. These enterprises are defined as new innovative firms engaged in knowledge transfer by demonstrating knowledge intensity in performing business activities and dealing with uncertainties to explore unique opportunities. KIEs operate in diverse sectors and are highly dependent on AI and human knowledge capital to analyze the cause and effects in business ecosystems by adapting to advanced technological platforms, market intelligence, and human resources to achieve competitive growth (Liu et al., 2022). The co-intelligence emphasizes human capital with advanced knowledge, adaptation, and practices in developing organization with competitiveness (Mudambi et al., 2018). These enterprises engage in developing complex portfolios with the support of AI in designing and delivering new products and services. Consequently, KIEs work with intellectual tasks that require a blend of AI, creativity, and need-based solutions as knowledge domains. The creation of co-intelligence and diffusion of knowledge are the central activities of KIEs to serve geo-demographic connectivity and develop inter- and intra-firm knowledge base for continuous innovation by playing a mediating role of technology within the industry. Entrepreneurial firms focus on wider market activities to stay competitive and serve geo-demographic needs by integrating people, products and services, innovation and technology, capital resources, performance, and knowledge flow. In addition, KIEs develop innovator connectivity (entrepreneurs contributing to new ideas), manufacturing and services connectivity, and build infrastructural accessibility for smooth transition of knowledge in diffusion and adaptation processes at various levels of business growth (Asmussen et al., 2019). The knowledge-intensive enterprises are often central to converge decision canvas with business canvas analyzing the NECTAR factors to grow competitive in the market with vertical (product mix) and horizontal dimensions (geodemographic expansion).

Case Studies

CS1: Commonwealth Bank

With the advancement of the concept of co-intelligence by converging AI-human interface in information pooling, data analytics, and decision making, the Commonwealth Bank of Australia (CBA) aimed at differentiating from its competing banks and improving the financial well-being of its customers. CBA is a leader in adopting an integrating AI throughout its banking operations with strategic focus to enhance customer experiences, streamlined operations and processes, improve security, and maintain a strong focus on responsible AI governance. The bank has been utilizing AI to deliver personalized and intuitive customer experiences through Customer Engine (CEE) and messaging through generative AI on various customer perspectives. CEE is powered by generative AI process to handle omni task decisions and provide hyper personalized services, which helps customers to access government benefits besides enhancing their banking experiences (Randazzo et al., 2023). The CEE was initially deployed in 2016, which was supported by an internal generative AI agent, ChatIT, to restructure conventional processes and reduce employee workload and provide agile workspace for fraud prevention security, and automated loan and credit reviews. The CEE has full cross-channel integration using many machine learning models from over 150 billion data points to deliver strong financial performance and supporting customers with self-service assistance packages to resolve problems remotely. The AI platforms commoditized key differentiators for attracting and retaining customers by ensuring speed, access, and value for money in bankable transactions (Lakhani et al., 2021).

One of the principal domains that were beneficial in adapting to AI support was to improve bank issued credit cards business where the customers had low satisfaction scores, cancellations, and occasional financial distress. Using the creative intelligence of behavioral economics team of the bank, this financial institution developed a plan to promote credit cards with less obvious drawbacks and stayed to improve customer choices (Buell & John, 2018). CBA has strategically partnered with leading technology providers to strengthen capabilities, reinforce decisions to improve customer services, and enhance internal competencies. Amazon web services have been integrated as cloud service providers while Microsoft supports the adoption of generative AI to strengthen cyber security and cloud platforms, like AZURE. Upon customers visiting the CBA branch, the CEE platform suggests options for the next best conversation (NBC) to the employees who greet customers. Accordingly, the employees use the conversation starters suggested by AI to improve the customer experience based on customer's requirements, feedback, and previous interactions. The NBC process has been adopted across all channels, which has shown encouraging results in conducting the next course of action. In addition, reviewing the behavioral economics, the bank sent various NBCs generated by AI to customers to test whether the CEE could help them make better decisions on fixing their personal issues like tax refunds. Such NBCs have been considered as an extra mile effort to develop customer relationship as social and personal concerns of bank toward customer's well-being (Randazzo et al., 2023).

The CEE allows CBA to make optimal use of data analytics to identify real-time customer needs and offer quick support as applicable solutions. The CEE has been a groundbreaking experience to bank and its customers integrating AI and human intelligence to improve the performance of front-line employees ahead of their competitors. The collaboration with AI-driven CEE improved bank's net promoter's code during COVID-19 pandemic period, which exhibited convincing lead in selling financial products of the bank. The core efficiency of CEE depended on explainability of AI-based predictions, training employees to develop efficiency within working teams, and developing most appropriate contents for delivering service messages to drive NBC prompts. The adoption of AI and application of CEE platform has been an effective transformational initiative of CBA to converge AI and human intelligence in financial entrepreneurship.

CS2: AI in Chinese Food Business

Food industry in China has a dynamic arena and has demonstrated the potential for continuous growth with technology, which has deployed AI across the value chain to address various challenges and revolutionize the food industry. Its hidden goal is farm-to-fork expansion by adapting to AI environment logarithms and AI-driven systems, in conjunction with the block chain technology. Most companies have employed AI-powered robots in food processing plants to ensure quality for consistency in human sensitive elements (vision, touch, taste, and smell) in Chinese ethnic foods (cured pork belly and black rice vinegar). The AI-driven systems monitor food storage and processing environments to overrule spoilage risks and ensure quality of the perishable products. Yum China, the key operator of KFC and Pizza Hut in the region, has deployed AI-powered system—iFS, which has been built upon their expensive food safety and quality control experience to minimize the risks in supply chain and food processing besides complying with the government regulations, media exposure, and control standards for animal pandemics.[2] The Yum China has also developed an AI-based system called eQA (electronic quality assurance) to manage the farm-to-fork process online through end-to-end digitized total quality management system in real-time. This enables also the Go-Go-Chicken project in tracking the chicken supplies from rural farms through block chain technology supported by AI and a combination of RFID and GPS.

The Yum China has applied the hub-and-spokes model in managing supply chain through a network of logistics centers and in-house supply chain management system central to transportation and warehousing. The company has adapted digital technologies including Internet-of-Things and AI to monitor products in real time, ensuring quality throughout the process. Responding to the client's feedback, the AI at Yum digital station has developed data analytics based on keywords of client statements such as expect, intend, predict, need, etc. Data analytics on such critical words enables the company to learn about consumer experience, perceptions, and historical trends in the real time context to support appropriate decision making. Adaptation to AI environment has been extended to the small food companies in China like Hanbao Foods (Hanbao refers to hamburger). This company is also a major supplier of hamburger buns to large western fast-food brands in China. This company has extended its business in health-oriented bakery products portfolio in view of the popularity of baked products in coffee and tea houses. The AI combined with e-commerce has significantly helped the company in catering to small clients by shifting the strategic approach to tactical gains (Dong et al., 2025).

[2]Yum China, 2022. Groundbreaking of New Supply Chain Management Center in Shanghai (https://ir.yumchina.com/news-releases/news-release-details/yum-china-announces-groundbreaking-new-supply-chain-management).

Continuous evolution of information and communication technologies (ICT) has significantly penetrated digitalization of conventional business processes and the Internet of Things (IoT) concept in business. The competitive engagement of firms with virtual technologies tends to unveil new business models (BMs) within hybrid environments. This phenomenon has extensively contributed to the continuous growth of new business economy in a hybrid environment. Such business impetus is developed around the so-called metaverses. In the cyber-physical ecosystem, BMs have been developed as a combination of physical- and virtual-world mechanisms that help in developing social and economic values. The economic creation and value capture at the crossroads of physical and virtual economies today are contributed through the cyber revolution comprising AI, AR, VR, and metaverse (Mancuso et al., 2023).

The food computing program has been associated with several major tasks including the food recognition, retrieval and recommendation. The food recognition has been AI-aided support involving the identification and classification of food items from visual data such as images and videos. This data has been beneficial to the food industry players in China for tracking nutritional objectives, food authentication, regulating food distribution in smart restaurants, and supermarkets besides managing the food waste (Karabay et al., 2025). Predicting the future implications of AI in Chinese food industry, it has been observed that upcoming start-ups in this segment are intending to implement omni solutions with a robot that can replace the human chef and manage stir fry, stew, add seasonings, and clean up by itself. Deploying the AI and digital technologies, Yum's China business is largely driven by rapidly growing middle-class consumer segment, which requires sustainable competitive advantages and real-time benefits in changing market scenarios. However, as consumers are increasingly attracted to not only healthy diets, but also enhance consumer experience with automation of services, which demands sentient AI-human interface from a large food supplier like Yum China.

References

Ahluwalia, S., Mahto, R. V., & Guerrero, M. (2020). Blockchain technology and startup financing: A transaction cost economics perspective. *Technological Forecasting and Social Change, 151.* https://doi.org/10.1016/j.techfore.2019.119854

Almgren, R., & Skobelev, D. (2020). Evolution of technology and technology governance. *Journal of Open Innovation: Technology, Market, and Complexity, 6*(2), 1–16.

Appio, F., Frattini, F., Petruzzelli, A., & Neirotti, P. (2021). Digital transformation and innovation management: A synthesis of existing research and an agenda for future studies. *Journal of Production and Innovation Management, 38*(1), 4–20.

Asmussen, C. G., Nielsen, B. B., Weatherall, C. D., & Lyngemark, D. H. (2019). Foreign ownership and global city characteristics: Unpacking the connectivity of micro-locations. *Regional Studies, 54*(3), 352–365.

Buell, R. W., & John, L. K. (2018). *Commonwealth Bank of Australia: Unbanklike experimentation.* Harvard Business Impact.

Çipi, A., Fernandes, R. D. A., Ferreira, F. A. F., Ferreira, C. M. Q. F. N., & Meidutė-Kavaliauskienė, I. (2023). Detecting and developing new business opportunities in society 5.0 contexts: A sociotechnical approach. *Technology in Society, 73.* https://doi.org/10.1016/j.techsoc.2023.102243

Dong, Y., Chen, J., Li, J., Zheng, Y., & Meng, Q. (2025). *Hanbao one's expansion strategy: Reaching small clients.* Harvard Business Impact.

Evangelista, R., Meliciani, V., & Vezzani, A. (2018). Specialisation in key enabling technologies and regional growth in Europe. *Economics of Innovation and New Technology, 27*(3), 273–289.

Giliyana, S., Bengtsson, M., & Salonen, A. (2025). Implementing and using smart maintenance technologies: Introducing challenges and enablers related to human, organizational and technological perspectives. *Procedia Computer Science, 253*, 932–941.

Gulawani, M. (2022). *MitiMeth: A Nigerian social Enterprise goes global.* Harvard Business Impact, Cambridge.

Holmström, J., & Hällgren, M. (2022). AI management beyond the hype: Exploring the co-constitution of AI and organizational context. *AI & SOCIETY, 37*, 1575–1585.

Huang, S., Wang, B., Li, X., Zheng, P., Mourtzis, D., & Wang, L. (2022). Industry 5.0 and society 5.0-comparison, complementation and co-evolution. *Journal of Manufacturing Systems, 64*, 424–428.

Karabay, A., Varol, H. A., & Chan, M. Y. (2025). Improved food image recognition by leveraging deep learning and data-driven methods with an application to central Asian food scene. *Scientific Reports, 15*, 14043.

Kim, R. Y. (2024). The fifth wave: The sustainability age and new industrial revolution. *IEEE Engineering Management Review*, 1–12. https://doi.org/10.1109/EMR.2024.3379036

Kliestik, T., Kral, P., Bugaj, M., & Durana, P. (2024). Generative Artificial Intelligence of Things Systems, Multisensory Immersive Extended Reality Technologies, and Algorithmic Big Data Simulation and Modelling Tools in

Digital Twin Industrial Metaverse Equilibrium. *Quarterly Journal of Economics and Economic Policy, 19*(2), 429–461.

Lakhani, K. R., Grushka-Cockayne, Y., Paik, J. H., & Randazzo, S. (2021). *Customer-centric design with artificial intelligence: Commonwealth Bank.* Harvard Business Impact.

Laland, K. N., Uller, T., Feldman, M. W., Sterelny, K., Müller, G. B., Moczek, A., Jablonka, E., & Odling-Smee, J. (2015). The extended evolutionary synthesis: Its structure, assumptions and predictions. *Proceedings of the Royal Society B Biological Sciences, 282.* https://doi.org/10.1098/rspb.2015.1019

Lee, J., Park, J., & Mostafa, N. A. (2025). Artificial intelligence dimensions and design features for the knowledge-based work of the future: A socio-technical perspective. *Data Science and Management.* https://doi.org/10.1016/j.dsm.2025.05.002

Liu, J., Zhou, H., Chen, F., & Yu, J. (2022). The coevolution of innovation ecosystems and the strategic growth paths of knowledge-intensive enterprises: The case of China's integrated circuit design industry. *Journal of Business Research, 144*, 428–439.

Ma, S., Zhang, Z., & Wan, Y. (2025, In press). An analysis of the path of labor protection in the innovation of small and medium-sized enterprises - a moderated mediation model. *International Review of Economics and Finance, 99.* https://doi.org/10.1016/j.iref.2025.104055.

Mancuso, I., Petruzzelli, A. M., and Panniello, U. (2023, in press). Digital business model innovation in metaverse: How to approach virtual economy opportunities. *Information Processing & Management, 60*(5). https://doi.org/10.1016/j.ipm.2023.103457

Meske, C., Bunde, E., Schneider, J., & Gersch, M. (2022). Explainable artificial intelligence: Objectives, stakeholders, and future research opportunities. *Information Systems Management, 39*, 53–63.

Mihai, S., Yaqoob, M., Hung, D. V., Davis, W., Towakel, P., Raza, M., Karamanoglu, M., Barn, B., Shetve, D., Prasad, R. V., Venkataraman, H., Trestian, R., & Nguyen, H. X. (2022). Digital twins: A survey on enabling technologies, challenges, trends and future prospects. *IEEE Communications Surveys & Tutorials, 24*(4), 2255–2291.

Moore, G. A. (2004). Darwin and the demon: Innovating within established enterprises. *Harvard Business Review.*

Moore, S. B., & Manring, S. L. (2009). Strategy development in small and medium sized enterprises for sustainability and increased value creation. *Journal of Cleaner Production, 17*, 276–282.

Mudambi, R., Li, L., Ma, X., Makino, S., Qian, G., & Boschma, R. (2018). Zoom in, zoom out: Geographic scale and multinational activity. *Journal of International Business Studies, 49*(8), 929–941.

Nagy, K., & Hajrizi, E. (2019). Building pillars for adapting society 5.0 in post-conflict countries. *IFAC-PapersOnLine, 52*, 40–45.

Papagiannidis, E., Mikalef, P., & Conboy, K. (2025). Responsible artificial intelligence governance: A review and research framework. *The Journal of Strategic Information Systems, 34*(2). https://doi.org/10.1016/j.jsis.2024.101885

PWC. (2025, May 28). *AI in Nigeria. Price water cooper.* https://tinyurl.com/AI-in-Nigeria

Rajagopal. (2024). Vertical integration and horizontal growth in entrepreneurship: Converging education, innovation, and technology ecosystems. In Rajagopal, M. Goncalves, & V. Zlatev (Eds.), *Entrepreneurship, innovation, and technology. Palgrave studies of entrepreneurship and social challenges in developing economies.* Palgrave Macmillan.

Randazzo, C., Scott, C. F., Bellini, R., Ammari, T., Devito, M. A., Semaan, B., & Andalibi, N. (2023). Trauma-Informed Design: A Collaborative Approach to Building Safer Online Spaces. In *Companion Publication of the 2023 Conference on Computer Supported Cooperative Work and Social Computing* (Minneapolis, MN, USA) (CSCW '23 Companion) (pp. 470–475). Association for Computing Machinery, New York, NY, USA.

Šmihula, D. (2010). Waves of technological innovations and the end of the information revolution. *Journal of Economy and International Finance, 2*, 58–67.

Tabibnia, G., & Radecki, D. (2018). Resilience training that can change the brain. *Consulting Psychology Journal: Practice and Research, 70*(1), 59–88. https://doi.org/10.1037/cpb0000110

Teo, S. A. (2025). Artificial intelligence, human vulnerability and multi-level resilience. *Computer Law & Security Review, 57.* https://doi.org/10.1016/j.clsr.2025.106134

Tumasjan, A., Braun, R., & Stolz, B. (2019). I gotta feeling: How twitter sentiment predicts venture capital valuations of technology startups. In *Academy of Management Proceedings.* https://doi.org/10.5465/AMBPP.2019.11887abstract

van Erkelens, A. M., Thompson, N. A., & Chalmers, D. (2024). The dynamic construction of an incubation context: A practice theory perspective. *Small Business Economics, 62*(2), 583–605.

Wang, K., Lu, Y., & Pan, Z. (2024). Understanding users' effective use of generative conversational AI from a media naturalness perspective: A hybrid SEM-ANN approach. *Data Science Management.*

Xu, X., Lu, Y., Vogel-Heuser, B., & Wang, L. (2021). Industry 4.0 and industry 5.0-inception, conception and perception. *Journal of Manufacturing Systems, 61*, 530–535.

Zhang, X., Zheng, J., Li, P., Yang, Y., Ye, Y., Causone, F., & Shi, X. (2025). A review of building digital twins: Framework and enabling technologies. *Journal of Building Engineering, 111.* https://doi.org/10.1016/j.jobe.2025.113117

Zu, X., Ni, G., & Hu, R. (2025). AI technology innovation, knowledge management and corporate environmental sustainability: Evidence from Chinese patent data. *Technology in Society, 83.* https://doi.org/10.1016/j.techsoc.2025.102984

CHAPTER 3

Technology and Human Factors

AI in Cognitive Ergonomics

Cognitive ergonomics in entrepreneurship connects the mental aspects of entrepreneurs explaining their interactions with systems, processes, and technological scenarios over the conventional wisdom. It exhibits collaborative and cognitive abilities by using technology platforms and AI to exercise co-intelligence. Cognitive ergonomics in entrepreneurship is a part of mind mapping synchronized with AI and ML to analyze perceptions, episodic memories, dynamic scenarios, and decision making by integrating human performance with technology-driven processes. The use of AI and ML in refurbishing cognitive blocks among entrepreneurs enables them to reorient cognitive abilities to optimize cognitive functions and functional efficiency. Cognitive ergonomics aims to optimize entrepreneurial workload by designing systems that are intuitive, easy-to-learn and practice, and require minimum cognitive efforts (Gualtieri et al., 2022). The use of AI delimits the cognitive barriers and minimizes potential errors by customizing design systems to reduce the likelihood of errors. Cognitive ergonomics is also affected by workplace design, which helps in focusing on task management and reducing distractions, improving information flow, and supporting effective entrepreneurial decision making. Entrepreneurial ergonomics has an outgrowth of entrepreneurial

Rajagopal, A. Rajagopal, *Artificial Intelligence and Entrepreneurship*, Palgrave Studies of Entrepreneurship and Social Challenges in Developing Economies,
https://doi.org/10.1007/978-3-032-14904-6_3

cognition, which helps in structuring tasks implementation and managing repetitive tasks by engaging AI to promote efficiency in complex task scenarios. The AI-driven entrepreneurial ergonomics extends to mental and emotional well-being of the entrepreneur by promoting healthy work-life balance. Implementing entrepreneurial ergonomics strategy proactively creates co-intelligent work environment and practices, which support strategic well-being and productivity in entrepreneurial business (Kolbeinsson et al., 2019).

The advancements in information and communication technology enable significant transition of socio-technical thinking between entrepreneurial concepts and business modeling. The growing effects of co-intelligence in AI-human interface has contributed to cognitive strengths among entrepreneurs in developing meticulous solutions analyzing problems, needs, and expected solutions (PNS) factors on various business scenarios. The application of generative and predictive AI has exhibited a wide array of synchronous solutions embedding versatility, dexterity, speed, and accuracy in managing scenarios. Such co-intelligence enabled automation processes in industries of various sizes and scales of production through collaborative and managerial strategies, which helped in overriding conventional approaches in entrepreneurship. Consequently, AI and technology platforms have revolutionized Industry 5.0, Entrepreneurship 5.0, and Society 5.0. Such technology revolution has driven cyber-physical system, flexibility, and safety in industrial and business modeling to reform cognitive ergonomics to help synchronous (real-time) managerial decision making (Kolbeinsson et al., 2019).

The cognitive synergy between AI and human intelligence has been bridged by increasing capabilities and competencies in enhancing creativity, problem solving, and decision-making. However, it is globally debated that the role of AI should augment cognitive synergy and reform cognitive ergonomics but not replace the human intelligence and entrepreneurial collaborations. The contribution of AI has been widely recognized in excelling complex data analytics, identifying embedded patterns, and automating repetitive tasks without interfering the human creativity, intuitions, and complex reasoning skills. The substantial engagement of entrepreneurs with AI-enabled devices significantly accommodated the subjective rationale, emotions, and implementing experience-based designs to gain sustainable competitive advantages (Khanra et al., 2020). Sociologists and anthropologists had a long debate on nurturing entrepreneurship through social networks and socio-cultural factors, which has been narrowed down by individual traits on using AI and developing isolated actions to manage resources, information, and entrepreneurial plans. The rise of generative AI has made a dynamic impact on entrepreneurial practices by leveraging AI and ML interactions to gain competitive advantage by distinguishing the business models and innovations to match with the emerging market dynamics. The augmentation and enhancement of human intelligence and capabilities in collaboration with AI has widely addressed the perspectives of co-intelligence and hybrid intelligence where the two entities collaborate in analyzing the SWOT (strength, weakness, opportunity, and threats) attributes of cognitive outcome, capabilities, and competencies (Haleem et al., 2022). Building on the notion of AI-based cognitive augmentation, enterprises of various scales have contributed to value creation, innovative business ventures, and competitive business models to cater to the NOISE (need, opportunities, innovation, strength, and expectation).

AI has emerged as an open collaborative partner than a disruptive technology, which encourages human cognitive potential, insights, and judgments to gain real-time advantage in exploiting opportunities and enhancing the potential capabilities to match with dynamic market trends and consumer preferences by making creative decisions. The data-driven insights significantly support entrepreneurial decision making despite the limitations of AIs planning-based models in uncertain business scenarios. Accordingly, the combination of AI and cognitive neural networks generate valuable starting points for business inquiries, which can be explored through data-based computational methods to develop entrepreneurial precision in decision making (Artz & Ren, 2025). Behavioral process is supported by the consumer's perceived value emerging out of the economic benefits and risk analysis in using technology-based sustainability products and services. The behavioral process stage leads to the defensive behavior stage by critical evaluation of needs, awareness, and their fit into the values and lifestyle. The stage that follows defensive-behavior stage drives consumers to justify their perceptions and attitude toward green decisions and optimize output. Most people at this stage seek social validation and reward for their decision to stay with the sustainable products and tend to lead environmental advocacy and green leadership at niche and regional levels of society. However, as social consciousness grows, self-actualization on sustainability commitments increases (Rajagopal, 2024). Collective intelligence (CI)-led business models rely more on consumer preference and social criteria while evaluating the ideas that are generated through open innovation. Successful crowdsourcing ventures require more than an online platform and some kind of brand connection. Without an understanding of participant motivations and behaviors, casual attempts to leverage the wisdom of the crowd may backfire and lead to unintended results. Prominent examples of crowdsourcing failures are myriad. Consider General Motors, which provided users with web tools to make their own ads for the Chevrolet Tahoe, resulting in a number of viral videos that lampooned the company's products and the American automotive industry's gas guzzlers more generally. In the fast-moving consumer goods industry, Mountain Dew successfully crowdsourced part of its product development through the Dewmocracy contest series, but a similar project asking fans to name the brand's new apple-flavored drink brought on a slew of ironic suggestions, including Diabeetus (Fedorenko et al., 2017).

Technological evolution is independent of social and economic factors, but, over the years, it has been streamlined with purpose to impact society and industry as illustrated in Fig. 3.1. Consequently, technological evolution has been streamlined with purpose of developing technologies for social development, increasing industrial productivity and performance, and supporting radical innovation, which significantly disrupts the business processes with the purpose of value creation. The growing social and industrial technologies have led to transforming cognitive ergonomics among entrepreneurs by substituting the conventional wisdom with co-intelligence (AI-human interface), which has changed the social and technological thinking among entrepreneurs to develop sustainable and

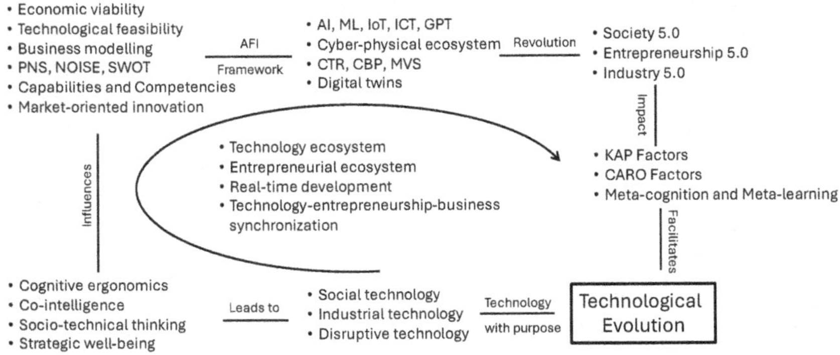

Fig. 3.1 Technological evolution and its effects. (Source: Authors)

strategic well-being. These factors have significantly influenced the market-oriented innovation by ensuring economic viability and technological feasibility to develop competitive business models and nurture market-oriented innovation. The effective use of technology in entrepreneurial business requires thorough analysis of PNS, NOISE, and SWOT factors. Accordingly, entrepreneurs need to enhance their capabilities and competencies in integrating technology to develop competitive business models and achieve entrepreneurial leadership. Entrepreneurs require a systematics and strategic approach using **a**nalysis, **f**ormulation, and **i**mplementation (AFI) to develop competitive entrepreneurship. The AFI framework can be integrated with AI, ML, IoT, information and communication technology (ICT), and general-purpose technology (GPT) to strengthen cyber-physical ecosystem, which may also nurture the applications of digital-twins in technology-driven enterprises. However, the AFI framework needs to be analyzed at micro level in the context of CTR, capital-benefit-performance (CBT), and minimum viable segment (MVS) to develop micro, small, and medium enterprises holistically.

The use of AFI framework across the above discussed factors has revolutionized society 5.0, entrepreneurship 5.0, and industry 5.0, which developed symbiosis across these segments with advanced applications of technology leading to higher productivity and performance as exhibited in Fig. 3.1. Technological evolution has significantly influenced the KAP and CARO factors besides developing meta-cognition and meta-learning capabilities among entrepreneurs. These factors have also led to significant impact in leading the technological revolutions across society, entrepreneurship, and industry. The transforming entrepreneurial cognition is largely driven by the changing technology ecosystem with focus on synchronous (real-time) development to streamline technology, entrepreneurship, and business operations.

Cognitive ergonomics of entrepreneurs is widely based on trust and validity, which is outgrown from the experiential knowledge. However, engaging AI in cognitive and emotional changes is often validated by the experiential knowledge and trust of entrepreneurs through a rational assessment of the capabilities and performance of co-intelligence (Fletcher et al., 2019). Entrepreneurs develop cognitive trust upon using the AI system parallel to their **k**nowledge, **a**daptability, and **p**ractice experiences (KAP) in the context of **c**onsistency, **a**ccuracy, **r**eliability, and **o**utput (CARO). The perceived reliability and accuracy in cognitive ergonomics of entrepreneurs while using AI system is largely affected by KAP and

CARO variables, which tend to match the AI-driven entrepreneurial cognition with positive experiences and critical success factors. The transparency and explainability in AI-adapted cognitive ergonomics of entrepreneurs tend to validate the CARO variables with KAP factors to generate cognitive trust. The AI-adapted cognitive ergonomics enhances individual competencies in the context of KAP through accurate predictions, effective problem-solving processes, and achieving successful outcomes. Building cognitive trust widely depends on analyzing contents of co-intelligence offering transparency, managing expectations, and focusing on accuracy and reliability through logical interpretations, physical validity, monitoring, and feedback mechanisms (Richert et al., 2018).

Continuous evolution of information and communication technologies (ICT) has significantly driven digitalization of conventional business processes and the concept of Internet of Things (IOT) in business. The competitive engagement of firms with virtual technologies tends to unveil new business models (BMs) within hybrid environments. This phenomenon has extensively contributed to the continuous growth of the new business economy in a hybrid environment. Such business impetus is developed around the so-called metaverses. In the cyber-physical ecosystem, BMs have been developed as a combination of physical- and virtual-world mechanisms that help in developing social and economic values. Reviewing changing technological perspectives, Artificial Intelligence (AI) is often considered the 'fifth wave' of computing, signifying a major transformative technological advancement that is currently shaping various industries and aspects of life, characterized by autonomous AI systems capable of operating independently in complex environments. Economic creation and value capture at the crossroads of physical and virtual economies today are enabled through the cyber revolution comprising AI, AR, VR, and metaverse. BMs based on digital technologies and within hybrid environments are becoming increasingly popular to facilitate innovative products and services offerings, collaborations, and transactions through new interaction modalities within community-based and crowd-based contexts. Therefore, virtual BMs are challenging and innovating the traditional market dynamics, which not only augments profit, but also helps in managing unforeseen business conditions. Consequently, firms implementing virtual business models have been successful in reducing the cost, time, and risk factors in business and enhancing market-oriented innovations in digital and virtual environments.

Artificial Intelligence and machine language (ML) technologies have revolutionized managerial decision making through interactive platforms, which are transforming the decision-making processes by inducing advanced learning capabilities. The convergence of AI and ML are highly personalized, based on manager's interest in resolving organizational conflicts and making decisions through AI platforms. A pre-trained model of AI and ML helps in developing a logical framework with a large amount of verbal and non-verbal data to enable decision making in a highly sophisticated manner. The advanced capabilities of AI and ML allow managerial decisions to administer situation-based decisions by matching problems, needs, and solutions. However, the impact of ChatGPT as an outgrowth of AI and ML has limited implications in complex business situations, as Artificial Intelligence offers large number of options which can be categorized as choice overload in managerial decisions. Managerial decision making conventionally depends on organizational knowledge, intelligence, and culture, which affects the cognition process at both the managerial and organizational levels. Previous studies have shown that superimposing technology on managerial decision making often does not match with the intellectual bandwidth of managers and stakeholders in deriving the sense of commonality. Therefore, synchronizing meta-cognition and meta-learning is a major challenge in technology-based decision making, and making decisions compatible with tangible and quantifiable improvements.

Technological Empowerment

The contemporary growth of individual entrepreneurs and community entrepreneurship is largely based on the adoption of technological and adaptation to changing environment. Political philosophy, power, economy, and governance in developing economies are collectively responsible to empower entrepreneurs with technology adoption to enhance individual and group capabilities enabling them to improve productivity and performance to achieve socio-economic well-being. Technological empowerment (TE) requires ensuring entrepreneurs regardless of their socio-economic status to have access to technology and appropriate skills to use it. Such empowerment offers tools and resources, which enable entrepreneurs to learn, communicate, and perform tasks efficiently and effectively within the technological environment (Frick et al., 2021). TE helps entrepreneurs in systematic decision making to pursue their goals and achieve market competitiveness through technology-led business modeling. Leveraging technology, individual and community entrepreneurship, can address collectively the social and economic challenges and foster growth in business and economic values. TE can further be extended to ensure inclusivity and diversity to benefit entrepreneurs with disability and socio-economic diversity. However, it is important to promote ethical use of technology including data privacy, security, and non-imitability. The impact of TE can be measured with selective social and economic key performance indicators aligned with individual and community goals (Wang & Su, 2021). TE has been visual in digital transformation of local entrepreneurship while it has shown a positive impact on corporate performance toward environmental, social, and governance (ESG). TE and digital transformation are essential drivers of both entrepreneurial and corporate competitiveness driven by optimal resource use, enhanced efficiency, and market-led innovation. The digital transformation in the context of AI and ML has redefined entrepreneurial business models and operational processes leading to higher efficiency and competitiveness.

TE has significantly contributed to improving entrepreneurial knowledge and skills in adapting to digital technology, improving productivity and performance, and overcoming various business dilemmas caused by non-conformity and cognitive resistance. The entrepreneurial development centers in developing economies like India, have given upthrust to TE to modernize entrepreneurial development and business governance through economic value management. Consequently, digital technologies have significantly enhanced the efficiency of local enterprises and resolved the conventional decision-choice conflicts in managing entrepreneurship and business. Digital technology is central to IoT, Big Data, AI, and cloud computing with advanced fifth generation information and communication technology, which enables entrepreneurial performance through technological efficiency. The deep integration of TE and digital technologies in individual and community entrepreneurship has improved market-based innovations, process simplifications, and value co-creation among enterprises, stakeholders, and consumers. Consequently, the unification of TE, entrepreneurship, and market has significantly promoted the people-centered approach to promote entrepreneurial efficiency, quality, and inherent social values. The successful adaptation and creation of technology-based entrepreneurial ventures are significantly influenced by the interactions within social networks (tradition and digital), which augment the ability to create collective intelligence, and environmentally and socially integrated economic systems. Technology-led business models are largely driven by the social networks and stakeholders at the mature stage of business as they rely more on social patronage and values than corporate sponsorship. However, the development of such business models is a complex process that requires a supportive entrepreneurial and social ecosystem (Neumeyer & Santos, 2018).

The policy of TE needs to be combined with entrepreneurial incubation to develop knowledge and skills in adapting to technological environment and streamlining the processes with the business dynamics. Incubation of innovations has emerged as a new model of start-up facilitation in most developing economies. Venture capitalists review the incubators and assess the projected growth and profitability in businesses to invest. They review the incubators to diversify risky investment portfolios, while the prospecting entrepreneurs approach the incubators to review the economically viable and technologically feasible support for start-up projects. Entrepreneurial incubators face both challenges and opportunities to grow into competitive enterprises considering the embedded investment and entrepreneurial risks. Broadly, there are five incubator archetypes such as the university incubator, the independent commercial incubator, the regional business incubator, the company-internal incubator, and the virtual incubators. The major problems associated with implementing the TE-entrepreneurship alignment among micro, small, and medium firms are as discussed below (Rajagopal, 2021):

- Risk and uncertainty: Size of the firm, organizational design, infrastructure, and knowledge on environmental issues
- Technological factors: Complexity of technology, sustainability initiatives, transfer of technology, cost, and technology lifecycle
- Public policies: Governance of public policies, regulations and standards, social responsiveness
- Market barriers: Product attractiveness, pricing pressure, people, performance, psychodynamics, and absence of a long-term strategy
- Financial factors: Investment costs, payback, quality of service, and crowdfunding and government financial programs

Innovations in the emerging markets are sprouting through the manifold growth of start-up enterprises as an outcome of TE, which enables the enterprises to achieve market competitiveness and create value among stakeholders, consumers, and market players. Innovations in the emerging markets are conducted in both business-to-consumer and business-to-business segments that are being nurtured by sponsor companies to facilitate the innovation to commercialize and gain quick returns on innovations. Small start-up entrepreneurs in the emerging markets are working on the low-cost and sustainable innovations that deliver desirable results and enhance the perceived use value of the consumers. Accordingly, sustainable innovation is pacing fast in the emerging markets giving a major competitive challenge to the companies intending to penetrate high technology-high-cost innovative product in the above marketplace (Rajagopal, 2021).

Technology empowerment has three principal domains comprising community entrepreneurship, social perspectives, and operational factors as exhibited in Fig. 3.2. Community entrepreneurship is based on the engagement of individual or entrepreneurial groups taking innovative initiatives to gain competitive advantage in business to benefit local community by addressing PNS factors and fostering community well-being. Community enterprises prioritize social well-being over profit by serving as a driver of inclusive growth and social transformation (Raman et al., 2025). Technology empowerment enables entrepreneurs to develop ***awareness***, technology ***adaptation***, ***accessibility***, and ***alignment*** (A-4) with entrepreneurial tasks to develop technology-led business modeling embedding market-led innovation in entrepreneurial processes. Technology empowerment among entrepreneurs helps them in acculturation with AI, ML, and decision-making platforms, which enables digital transformation

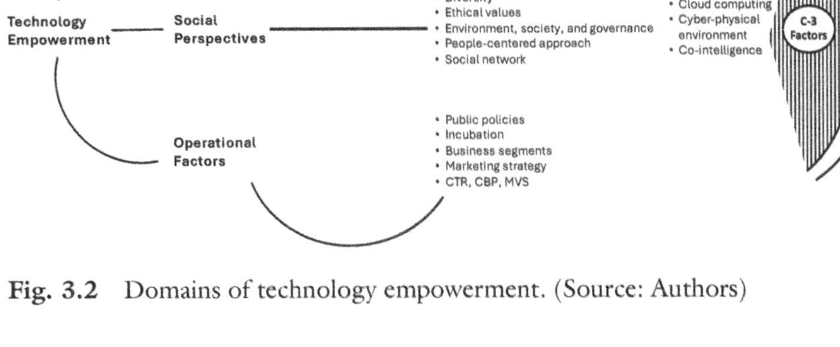

Fig. 3.2 Domains of technology empowerment. (Source: Authors)

in entrepreneurial functions. Technology empowerment helps entrepreneurs align themselves with several social perspectives such as entrepreneurial diversity, which allows individuals from varied backgrounds and experiences to contribute to entrepreneurial landscape. Consequently, entrepreneurial diversity contributes to attempting to complex creativity and gaining competitive advantage in the marketplace by converging social accelerator practices with dynamic market requirements (Shepherd & Gruber, 2021). Empowering technology in social domain leads to people-centered approach by enhancing social networks. The environment, society, and governance approaches are also benefitted by empowering society with technology to provide wider access and applicability within the framework of ethical values.

Public policies in both developed and developing countries empower entrepreneurs with the application of contemporary technologies to improve their capabilities and competencies and incubating innovative ideas to gain competitive advantage across business segments. AI and technology platforms help enterprises in deploying three distinctive mechanisms in the incubation process including initiating orchestrating and collaborating in the launch and development of entrepreneurial ventures (Liu, 2020). AI in technological platforms significantly supports the operational processes in entrepreneurial activities in resource planning, developing marketing strategies, and streamlining business operations. The use of AI in technology helps entrepreneurs in determining appropriate business segments such as business-to-business, business-to-consumers, consumer-to-consumer, and hybrid marketing segments. Technology also helps in reducing the CTR factors and enhancing CBP factors within the minimum viable segment. The diffusion and adaptation of technology is largely driven by the *cyber-physical* environment, *co-intelligence* (AI-human interface), and the efficiency of *cloud computing* (C-3 factors).

The digital marketing strategies with hybrid self-experience stations attract more consumers to experience the products online, develop and share experience, and measure the perceived use value (satisfaction) of the products. Hybrid self-experience stations are physical locations or platforms that seamlessly integrate both physical (in-person) and digital elements to provide an interactive, personalized, and self-directed user experience (Handke et al., 2024). Such web exposure for the product and services is accessible to many consumers today, which drives them to develop perceptions and attitude for the products and services of their choice. Artificial Intelligence and collective intelligence enhance and complement each other and together serve as a hybrid concept. Both require training in personal development and high performance. The hybrid collective intelligence process coordinates with Industry 4.0 management processes and encourages firms of various sizes and industries to learn together. Many proximity-based ideas have benefitted creative companies like LEGO, Samsung, and Sony (gaming division products) by reaching out to the crowd and communities. The dynamic attributes of crowdsourcing of these companies have ranged from localization to globalization, and disruption to hybridization. However, while implementing society-linked business models, companies tend to develop community hubs for customers and stakeholders to interact using face-to-face, digital, or hybrid communication models. The interactions of customers on these platforms help companies document the voice-of-customers to support strategy designs. Wisdom-of-crowd is a broad-spectrum cognitive pool, which contributes to collective intelligence with liberal thinking. Hybrid knowledge (a blend of conventional and technology-oriented knowledge) and group behavior have emerged as the principal source for firms to learn the perceptions of customers and stakeholders at large. The wisdom of crowd is motivated by the firms by creating a free space for thinking together on a predetermined topic. The digital networks and the enhanced scope of interpersonal meetings among peers have helped collective intelligence grow manifold over the years. The brainstorming in the crowd-cognition process categorically exhibits individual and group behavior (Hopf et al., 2024).

The ICT and AI complement the tourist knowledge, help in narrowing down the unveiled biases, and encourage eudaimonic behavior in adventure tourism. Adventure shopping enhances eudaimonic emotions, which is marginally different from perceived happiness or hedonic pleasure (George et al., 2021). However, when proximity products and services are commoditized, their benefits enormously serve the customer-centric firms. AI-based robots, unlike machines with predefined functions, could revolutionize the retail industry by offering interactive solutions. Cutting-edge technologies significantly affect the social and industrial development in transitional economies. The prominent technological edges that drive challenge-based research include Artificial Intelligence, augmented reality, virtual reality, wearable technology, robotics, and Big Data analytics. The growing environmental concerns, public policies, and scientific communities describe the efforts that utilize ecosystem processes to boost challenge-based research in engineering and technology to address societal challenges. The challenge-based research outputs have significantly contributed to the development of the consumer sector economy (Rajagopal, 2019).

Systems Thinking

Systems thinking has emerged as an approach to problem solving on dynamic business issues. As a process, entrepreneurs focus on understanding various parts of the scenario considering it as a holistic system and interact and influence within the organization. Consequently, systems thinking is an organizational process, which addresses complex internal issues through collective cognition and systematic approach to resolving dynamic business and management problems (Tobón & Luna-Nemecio, 2021). It interconnects AI and human scenarios to provide a contemporary approach to understand the causes and effects of problem scenarios and contribute through co-intelligence to the overall outcome. It emphasizes the relationship and interactions between internal capabilities and competencies as a system to analyze the impact of externalities and develop meta-knowledge recognizing the dynamic behavior of scenarios within organization. Systems thinking emphasizes that an organization is a dynamic entity and various factors influence organizational behavior, work culture, and values over time to adapt to the changes in organizational process and management (Linnéusson et al., 2025). It addresses complexity in cognition, resistance to change, and resilience with AI and technology to generate co-intelligence in managing organizational tasks. Considering the organization as an entire entity, systems thinking enables process innovation and explore new opportunities to develop organizational competitiveness facilitating the change and implementing new strategic orders to gain sustainability within the organization as a system (Kraus et al., 2021). It also helps in improving decision making by analyzing the decisions-conflicts-choices model to determine the effective cause and effect relationship to strengthen interconnectedness and manage organizational decisions, improve management practices, and work culture.

Systems thinking and process dynamics attempt to portray the performance-measurement system in marketing activities in a lucid way which has been an obscure issue for managers. A sound measurement system of various marketing operations in a firm improves decision-making scenario by focusing on the aspects of the market competition and core competencies of a firm to create organizational value and provide a valid and systematic justification for strategies implemented by the managers. System thinking is a managerial process of introspection of organizational culture in modulating contemporary strategy development, while process dynamics is a scientific approach to learn and penetrate complex business situations. There is an increasing interest among multinational companies in considering marketing operations to reengineer with precision the decision-making competencies by introducing systems thinking and process dynamics concepts.

The combination of AI with systems thinking enables a powerful decision support framework in enterprises of various sizes to navigate internal and external complexities and explore synergistic benefits including enhanced modeling, dynamic decision making, and cross-domain applications. AI enhances systems thinking by processing real-time data to support systems thinking and develop business models with predictive analytics, causal loop diagrams, and feedback-based improvement mechanisms to resolve complex internalities and externalities in entrepreneurial operations. The AI-human interface as a co-intelligence driver helps entrepreneurs in understanding iterative causes and effects and adaptation to such scenarios ensuring both contextual and holistic decisions. Systems thinking in combination with AI helps in making valuable decisions in both commercial and social enterprises such as innovative business modeling, healthcare management, supply chain streamlining, urban planning and developing competitive entrepreneurial strategy (Qudrat-Ullah, 2025). The organizational impact of systems thinking exhibits an organizational culture, which endorses resource-based view, co-intelligence, and data-driven insights supported by AI. Systems thinking provides ethical and strategic alignment across the stakeholders, employees, and business partners, and enables responsible AI implementation ensuring transparency and equity. Systems thinking interconnects business scenarios and broader entrepreneurial ecosystems to understand internal and external problems and develop a holistic approach to implement in inter- and intra-organizational work systems. Therefore, systems thinking penetrates deep into root causes and feedback loops for holistic problem solving instead of fixing isolated issues with low response on improvements. Entrepreneurs operate within networks of stakeholders, government, end-users, and business partners to coordinate with innovative ecosystems to achieve sustainable impact. Effective policy design, monitoring, and evaluation are also supported by systems thinking and entrepreneurship, which enables assessing entrepreneurial policies and their effectiveness through complex interactions and simulating scenarios with the help of AI (Chou, 2018).

Systems thinking and process dynamics concepts have emerged as a new stream of applications in mending conventional strategy development approach in marketing area. This is a holistic approach of monitoring, evaluation, and application process of appropriate marketing strategies, understanding the competition and its future implication on the business of a company. The emphasis of discussion is on the process of bringing systems into being, beginning with the identification of a need and extending through requirements determination, functional analysis and allocation, design synthesis, evaluation, validation, operation and support, phase-out, and disposal. By employing the iterative process of analysis, evaluation, feedback, and modification, most systems in existence can be improved in their affordability, effectiveness, and stakeholder satisfaction. Systems thinking, a part of operations and management research, essentially looks at the whole as a basis for understanding, designing, and managing its components that have convergence with management strategy and implementation. Systems thinking is applied in organizational management for decades in the field of operations but has been conceptualized also in the functional areas of marketing. Systems thinking offer a powerful new perspective, a synchronized flow of thoughts, and a set of tools that can be used to address the most complex problems in everyday business operations. Systems thinking may be considered as a way of understanding reality that emphasizes the relationships among various components in a process, rather than the independent constituents of the process. Based on a field of study known as system dynamics, systems thinking has a practical value that rests on a solid theoretical foundation.

The entrepreneurial advantages in implementing systems thinking in organizations inculcate strategic foresight, which enables entrepreneurs to leverage innovations at real-time. In addition, systems thinking fosters collaboration among diverse business partners and align stakeholders with the entrepreneurial policies to strengthen the entrepreneurial ecosystem. Businesses built with KAP and CARO elements and streamlined organizational systems stay better equipped to adapt to change and uncertainty in business. Systems thinking combined with AI and entrepreneurship manages automation of tasks by managing repetitive tasks and streamlines the focus on strategy. The generative AI helps with design thinking, product launch plans, website ergonomics, and marketing campaign with rapid prototyping to enable entrepreneurs to visualize and make right decisions.

The AI-linked systems thinking moderates market research and analytics across datasets to uncover trends, customer preferences, and competitive insights. In addition, AI lowers entry barriers by supporting entrepreneurs with optimal resources and bridging the human efficiency gaps (Brown, 2024).

Systems thinking as an idea can be applied in various scientific fields including, planning and evaluation, education, business and management, public health, sociology and psychology, cognitive science, human development, agriculture, sustainability, environmental sciences, ecology and biology, earth sciences, and other physical sciences. Systems thinking can influence many of the existing concepts, theories, and knowledge in each of these fields (Cabrera et al., 2008). In marketing and related business strategies, managers need to think ahead of competitors to keep moving from niche to market leader status. Changing the way we think does not automatically solve problems, issues, or crises in the business. However, systems thinking does reframe how we think about what we view as a problem in the first place, and what solutions might look like. The reasons for scientific utility and promise of systems thinking are extensive.

Human Factor and Artificial Intelligence

The rapid advancement of AI resources put conventional entrepreneurial management systems at the crossroads irrespective of the size of firm and scale of businesses. While large firms often engage in modernizing data platforms, upskilling analytics team and implementing AI-driven workflows to seek guidance from predictive AI, most micro level enterprises tend to use generative AI to support KAP and CARO factors in the entrepreneurial process. Market research, product design, manufacturing process, supply chain control, and delivering value through software environment are major contributions of AI to start-up entrepreneurs and large firms (von Krogh, 2018). AI-powered productivity tools are available in core platforms for product designing, process improvement, and customer relationship management, which is capable of tackling several challenges with the help of AI and data-driven enterprise resource systems (ERP). However, the risk and vulnerability in adapting to AI are increasing with third party providers who often control operational data and information security. Risk governance and oversight of diffusion of information with AI-based development program create vulnerabilities, data quality issues, and potential regulatory compliance gaps (Chalmers et al.,

2021). Consequently, it is important to develop human-in-the-loop reviews to validate AI output in the context of professional and business needs and regulatory constraints. Human-AI synchronization broadly results into co-intelligence, where AI moderate technology teams not only to develop cross-functional literacy but also to use the technology knowledge efficiently in the challenging areas. Developed countries have already initiated implementing fast-moving regulations, which applies to AI in the context of fiduciary duties, data protection, anti-fraudulence control, and consumer protection (PWC, 2025).

To effectively converge AI and human cognition, it is important to develop organizational leadership and structure team capabilities to align with the organizational strategies adopting to a problem first approach. Accordingly, entrepreneurs can adapt to the responsible AI and clarify intended impacts by enabling risk mitigation within organizational values and regulatory requirements. A scalable framework and organizational learning structure would help entrepreneurs to align with rapidly moving AI and robotics landscape. The human investment and knowledge and adaptation to AI among employees and clients must be subjected to the NOISE factors by analyzing *needs*, competitive *opportunities*, workflow *improvements*, organizational *strength*, and *expectations* for the use of responsible AI and expectations for high-quality outputs. Therefore, emerging enterprises must equip their teams with clear understanding of AI adaptability and associated risk factors to enable them to use AI tools in blending with culture and skills to drive innovation. Effective and ethical use of AI can transform entrepreneurial organizations by helping in decision-making, identifying real-time opportunities, and enhancing competitive performance. The co-intelligence extracted from generative AI and human experience impacts entrepreneurial firms by enhancing market competitiveness, accelerating innovation, improving outcomes, lowering influence of CTR factors, and increasing organizational performance. The human-AI interface serves as a powerful tool for creative problem solving and stakeholder empowerment through logical reasoning and response to disruptions (Shafiabady et al., 2024).

Architecting an effective AI-led enterprise, which complies with the requirements of technology infrastructure, is very essential besides identifying target audience, analyzing the existing market competition, setting-up clear goals, choosing right suppliers, and appropriate marketing channels. As the AI-support decision making enables user-efficient buying platforms, virtual store displays, order processing, and delivery management, it is important for the firms to optimize entrepreneurial performance across Internet-of-Things including search engine optimization (SEO) process. SEO efficiency can be enhanced by adding relevant keywords, meta descriptions, and structured data to improve search efficacy and search engine ranking. An efficient business-to-consumers website must be able to create compelling product pages, streamline the checkout process, implement personalized marketing tactics, and track results to make necessary adjustments. The key aspects of co-intelligence strategy include defining ways of brand positioning, pricing, promotions, and customer acquisition methods while leveraging social media and email marketing to engage audiences and reinforce their buying intentions. Radical changes in the consumer preferences due to disruptive technologies and frugal innovations, it is often challenging for the start-up enterprises to understand consumer demographics, needs, buying behaviors, and online buying behavior. Analyzing competitive strategies is another underlying challenge is to develop competitive decision dashboard with the help of AI to enable visual merchandising and develop differential marketing strategies (Rajagopal, 2025).

Visual merchandising in emerging enterprises is all about displaying products, features, reviews, and visual effects like action images and videos in a way that engages and persuades potential customers. To create visualization impact, every product in a category should have a homepage, which should be able to showcase window display of new products, bestsellers, and promotions to grab attention. In addition, the product home page must also showcase recommended products matching the attributes of the products and consumer search intentions. Showcasing recommended products can be based on generative Artificial Intelligence (AI) and consumer navigation data analytics. Using algorithmic model supported by AI and machine learning to suggest products based on a customer's browsing and purchase history can increase customer interaction and engagement with the products in the virtual merchandising ecosystem. Displaying complementary products together, like how outfits are displayed on mannequins in store, inspires customers to buy more than one item. Optimizing site layout to effectively showcase products is helpful to customers to conduct aimed navigation during the shopping journey. The intuitive navigation and personalized layouts enhance the user experience in online shopping and reinforce their interest in staying abreast with the competition. High-quality imagery and videos enhance consumer experience with products as use sharp, clear photos and videos stimulate the purchase intention of consumers and enable to reinforce the buying-decision. Showcasing products from 360° builds confidence, transparency, and trust on the products among consumers (Rajagopal, 2025).

To develop visualization on interrelated products and services, AI-supported firms should create semantics of core products like apple. The semantics of apple can be apple juice, apple jam, dehydrated apple, organic apple orchards, ethnic farming, apple vinegar, apple sider, and the like. Such semantics will help the firm in identifying the related products, processes, sustainability, and the associated ethnicity to display variety of products and attract consumers in navigation of the website. Semantics is fundamentally a study of meanings and etymologies in language which explores how words, phrases, sentences, and texts convey meaning and build contextual relationships. Semantics examines the meaning of words and how these meanings combine to form the meanings of sentences and larger texts, which involves understanding senses and references in the relationship between expressions and the products they refer to. Data visualization has some key elements including clear purpose, attractive contents including competitive advantages and use values associated with the products, structure of the visualization framework, organized sequential format to arrange placeholders with comments, and neural design that could inculcate emotions and stimuli among the consumers and liberal website navigators. Among many decorative, representative, mnemonic, organizational, relational, transformational, and interpretive visuals for the core categories, mnemonic visuals are images or diagrams used to help remember the information by associating it with visual cues. These tools are particularly effective for people to learn from visuals and develop perceptions and can help recall information to support contextual decision making. Mnemonic visuals work by linking an image with the information you need to remember (Rajagopal, 2025).

Artificial Intelligence (AI) in marketing has a new space to grow in the customer-centric firms. AI has gone beyond robotics structures for the customers as it is now emerging as a tool for decision making among consumer-oriented firms. Coding multiple information and communication technologies (ICT) have been central to the value creation and have provided efficient services for enhancing consumers' experiences. AI is now able to manage data analysis and deliver managerial decisions to the tourism firms. However, human element is not totally replaced with machines in managing firms. AI is integrated with ICTs to be omnipresent in all stages of a tourist's journey, and supports the ecstasy of customers

(Buhalis et al., 2019). Early in this century, social robots played a pivotal role in serving the social institutions and tourism industry to disseminate information and converse with humans. Broadly, Alexa and Siri are also accommodated as social robots with AI to interact with humans. Generative AI is driving revolution in the public domain to develop interactive relationships and mutual dependency to learn and widen the information silos. AI robots serve as co-workers and analysts for decision making in large multi-brand and international customer-centric firms. AI has yet to support tourism and hospitality industry robots with trust, anticipation, and emotions. Happiness, arousal, and merriment have a significant impact on robot sentiment polarity, while anticipation and surprise do not significantly affect the AI logarithms. Therefore, one major challenge is to anthropomorphize robots for tourism and hospitality industry (Jörling et al., 2019).

Disruptive Technologies and Entrepreneurial Mindset

Disruptive technologies have been strongly influenced by the needs and expectations for competitive advantages in markets and business. The disruptive innovation theory argues that technological disruption is a needed effort to override conventional practices and develop new entrepreneurial practices, business paradigms, and develop values to match with entrepreneurial mindset and experience. Accordingly, techno-social disruptions play a major role in reconceptualizing social and economic factors in entrepreneurial activities to gain competitive advantage and develop integration with market and entrepreneurial process (Liu et al., 2020). The disruptive technologies leading to competitive innovations enable entrepreneurs to create a new market by improving the existing products/services, which are on the verge of *end-of-life*. The performance of disruptive technologies can be measured through performance matrix and mainstream customer value. For instance, Amazon has been disruptive in e-commerce entrepreneurship with respect to continuously transforming the business models in logistics, display in virtual store, and connecting to customers with suppliers. The disruptive entrepreneurship can be broadly regarded as a development of new manufacturing or service domains with low inclination toward the conventional entrepreneurial practices (Carlsen et al., 2010). This can be explained with an example of Uber as non-disruptive technology in entrepreneurship in the taxi market as this service is a platform-based improvement over the conventional domain. The disruptive innovation companies, upon successful development of prototypes, backward linkages, and innovation collaborations can introduce radical products in competitive markets. Such innovations face the challenge in market testing to manage segmentation, targeting, and positioning of disruptive products (Rajagopal, 2023).

Artificial Intelligence enables entrepreneurial practices toward disruptive changes and develops interactive frameworks to lead cognitive shifts in developing innovations on new domains. The cognitive shifts with AI represent co-intelligence in developing disruptive technologies in local entrepreneurial markets by improving business models and restructuring organizational culture. The co-intelligence helps entrepreneurs in multitasking and integrating systems thinking in entrepreneurial process. However, AI-based disruptive innovation needs continuous attention, multi-tasking, and cognitive dependence to manage digital tools and streamline focusing on production and processes. Cognitive dependence tends to rely on technologies like cloud computing in memory-based navigation to streamline the AI-human interface and entrepreneurial processes (Schot & Steinmueller, 2018). Consequently, social and entrepreneurial shifts often challenge disruptive technologies based on ethical evaluation, process complexities, and overlapping entrepreneurial intelligence. Entrepreneurs often fear that AI leads to creating a dystopia (ambiguity and dissatisfaction) working with machine language overriding the entrepreneurial wisdom. However, AI has emerged as a technological similarity, which is growing exponentially overtaking entrepreneurial creativity and disrupting the societal values. On the contrary, pro-AI entrepreneurial advocacy reinforces the notion that AI is enabling co-intelligence and working in tune with the entrepreneurial mindset to improve manufacturing, logistics, services, and decision-making abilities (Gobble, 2016).

AI is transforming various entrepreneurial sectors despite the fear of replacing humans with robots and reducing human intervention in processes of various services. Automation of entrepreneurial operations provides tactical gains against strategic, entrepreneurial work model with human involvement. However, a large number of firms including start-up ventures argue that the biggest performance of AI is toward improvement in design thinking, reducing the human errors in manufacturing, and enhancing the information analysis. The AI agents, therefore, contribute to redesigning business processes, improving operational agility, speed, and scalability, besides stimulating real-time decision making (Wilson & Daugherty, 2018). Accordingly, entrepreneurial mindset needs to be aligned with the use of AI by developing employee orientation and effective human-machine interface. Scaling up entrepreneurship with AI should involve the following steps (Fountaine et al., 2021):

- Identifying a potential area to interconnect entrepreneurial activities and opportunities by sharing technology, reducing CTR factors, and aligning with the social PNS factors to gain competitive advantage
- Exploring AI to analyze NOISE factors in the context of entrepreneurial skills, market requirements, and operational efficiency
- Forming effective teams with right people by developing clear entrepreneurial projects and using AI to overcome the potential problems encountered in entrepreneurial business model
- Restructuring business models integrating AI to reinforce key success factors and organizational changes to align with the agile entrepreneurial mindset

The current state of human-machine interaction can be identified as Hybridization 4.0, which explains the 4th level of human-technology interface with AI as an effective and advanced cognitive enabler. The Hybridization 4.0 enables extension of human cognitive abilities leading to cyber-physical identity, anthropomorphizing human-AI interface, and meeting pragmatic challenges in entrepreneurial processes (Babushkina & Votsis, 2022).

Contemporary entrepreneurs explore their manufacturing and marketing operations within the predetermined entrepreneurial clusters, which help them in understanding the consumer behavior and market preference, and gaining insights from the entrepreneurial guild toward developing appropriate business models. These clusters serve as hubs for attracting potential investors, developing an entrepreneurial networking platform, and evaluating strengths and weaknesses. The role of such entrepreneurial guilds is critical, as it provides a platform for micro, small, and medium enterprises to gain investors' confidence and create value from the network members, which stimulates venture capitalists, angel investors, and potential consumers. The revolutionary concepts like 'dark kitchen' have significantly altered the conventional mindset of consumers who have transformed the focus of their entrepreneurial operations with growth-oriented strategy driven by agility, creativity, and innovation (Hakim et al., 2022).

The transformed mindsets have also raised the opportunity for disruptive innovations to attract customers over the existing products and services. However, such radical entrepreneurial attributes are often far from conventional practices, which focus on differential advantages and cater to asymmetrical consumer preferences by establishing unique sales propositions to support disruptive innovations. The new entrepreneurial mindset encourages entrepreneurs to develop innovative products and services on predetermined business canvases to facilitate the delivery of innovative products to end users effectively. The current trends of micro businesses engaged with micro, small, and medium enterprises, evolve around the PNS factors, which are cocreated by engaging stakeholders, gatekeepers, and industry sponsors. Such innovations have low cost of production, which enable entrepreneurs to deliver the products at competitive prices. The entrepreneurial mindset in the changing consumer preferences is driven by sustainability and social consciousness. Constructivism is one of the strongest capabilities of the entrepreneurial thought process. Constructivism focuses on motivations, curiosity, quick processing of information, creativity, risk appetite, teamwork, and practical approach toward innovation and technology (Rajagopal, 2023).

The penetration of digital technology and disruptive innovation have radically changed the social engagement of entrepreneurs to foster contemporary skills and analyze the role of the individual entrepreneurship in the context of corporate entrepreneurship. Traditionally, entrepreneurship was founded as a driver to improve social economy and deliver benefits to the stakeholders from the perspective of social welfare and well-being. The altered foundation of entrepreneurship is market-oriented and demands significant investment toward innovation and technology to develop market competitiveness. However, adjusting with social and ethical values seems to be a major challenge in connecting local enterprises with global businesses and induce effective social change alongside the business model. Therefore, it is necessary to redefine the means to overcome conventional social challenges by converging the entrepreneurial efforts with contemporary business and marketing philosophies. In the context of digital entrepreneurship, developing social initiatives are largely based on industry attractiveness comprising the extent of competition triggered by new entrants, the expected effects of substitution of products and services, and the bargaining power of consumers and suppliers at both ends of entrepreneurs and marketers (Battisti, 2019; Rajagopal, 2023).

Transformation of conventional entrepreneurship to hybrid entrepreneurial organizational design is a long journey of design thinking from traditional approach through market ecosystem. Digitalization in manufacturing and marketing has played a significant role in driving entrepreneurship through the transformational phase from conventional to contemporary entrepreneurial system. This has helped in conceptualizing the innovation and exploring opportunities through the interphase between entrepreneurs and market forces by linking organized entrepreneurs and their operational environment. The entrepreneurial journey has transformed from tangible and intangible mediums to continuous learning and adapting based on the philosophy of knowing, doing, and being to explore opportunities and create value in the changing market dynamics (Rajagopal, 2023). The radical conceptualization and organized design thinking both have significantly contributed to exploring the opportunities and resolving the PNS factors from the perspectives of customers. However, the lack of systematic understanding of the availability of competitive opportunities and the existing gaps have created complexities in establishing design locus in the context of dynamic preferences of customers and market demand. Consequently, developing entrepreneurial business models in tune to the radical market shifts and digitalization requires consortium strategy integrating homogeneous enterprises than designing individual enterprises to gain market competitiveness. Transforming the entrepreneurship from a design thinking perspective with future-oriented approach is a recursive process, which needs to be driven from the perspective of continuous shifts in market and consumption ecosystems (Berglund et al., 2020).

Case Studies

CS1: Cobalt Robotics—Replacing Workplace Humans

Conventionally, companies spend a huge amount on industrial security as it is critical to manufacturing, processing, supply chain and logistics, and services segment firms. With the increasing wage structure and labor rights complications, affording human security guards for many companies has been expensive besides the high turnover of personnel providing industrial security guards. One of the principal reasons for turnover is due to the isolated and repetitive nature of job, which often created job-based stress and frustration. Understanding the problems, needs, and expected solutions for industrial safety, Cobalt's robots have emerged as a great help to the companies. Cobalt Robotics is a young enterprise, built around the AI environment has been founded in 2016 in Fremont, California.[1] It is a company with a service acronym as RaaS, which explains its objectives and workspace environment as Robot-as-a-Service, built with autonomous workspace robots, which were designed to replace or supplement human security guards. The Cobalt robots could work round the clock managing repetitive work and exhibiting accuracy. Cobalt had deployed hundreds of security robots in companies across countries including DoorDash, Yelp, FedEx, and Ali Finance. The clients of this company are typically business corporations with strong commitment to automation and technology, besides corporate environments including offices, data centers, high tech facilities, and campuses.

Cobalt Monitoring Intelligence (CMI) is an advanced security platform designed to empower security for both inside and outside operations with the AI teams possessing high capabilities and precision to override human oversight. CMI seamlessly integrates its operations within the client's infrastructure and enhances security operations by reducing noise, optimizing workflows, and providing actionable solutions in real time. The CMI includes AI-powered alarm filtering with the capability of AI-led processing the alarm data while the video feeds provide the context for evidence-based decision making. The real-time threat detection under various scenarios, instant verification, and action to support automated actions such as guard communication and dispatches using AI and human-in-the-loop processes are also delivered by CMI. Comprehensive root cause analysis and seamless integration with customization and operational scalability provide a comprehensive view on real-time dashboards to serve prompt decision making (Rayport et al., 2023). Though Cobalt is a high AI-driven security company, there exists a series of challenges and pending decisions around how to scale business and how to overcome the human-AI impact factor. Such complexities have hindered the Cobalt robots from reaching expected targets through predetermined distribution channels. Consequently, the company envisioned penetrating other workplace robotic functions beyond security and scale its business through go-to-market strategy.

[1] For details on Cobalt AI company please refer https://www.cobaltai.com/

Cobalt Command Center (CCC) offers powerful remote security monitoring combining AI-driven analytics and human judgment with actionable insights, real-time threat detection, and scalable solutions. Human-in-the-loop process is managed by skilled workers who verify the AI-generated alerts and suggest actionable solutions in real-time. It is a co-intelligence process, where human cognition and insights help in identifying the AI misinterpretations and improve the accuracy and reliability. This process is further supported by the comprehensive data insights and reporting system, which monitors the events and lapses, and provides an aggregated analysis with actionable recommendations. Accordingly, the company enhanced its mission as *help people do more work that matters*, beyond the focus on security and collaborative workplace solutions for the future. During the initial period, the company faced resistance from segments of security personnel as the company intended to replace human security with AI and machine learning–based security robots. In view of such social demonstrations, the company has determined to follow the go-to-market strategy using both direct and indirect sales approach. The indirect approach is intended to sell robots through contract security companies, commercial malls, and real estate management companies. However, direct selling through channel partners offered potential for faster growth to the company without dwelling in controversies. The Cobalt company also integrated major elevator and door companies to use robots without human intervention to operate across different floors and open doors. The major competitors to this company appeared over time in the AI robotics market included *Knightscope*, *Boston Dynamics*, and *SMP* robotics operating with similar segmentation, targeting, and positioning strategies in the market.

The go-to-market strategy of the company has been based on two sales channels—direct sales and sales through distribution channels. The company used the former channel to sell security services direct to end users. Besides these channels, the company also perceived an indirect sales channel of selling security robots through the security guard companies, which have specialized on security needs assessment and delivering expected solutions. While operating through the distribution operation model, the company relied on the channel partners to educate clients on Cobalt Solutions and develop customer relationship for strategic sales and service. In this AI-based robotic entrepreneurial venture, the company faced challenges at the security personnel level and at the employee level. The replacement of humans with security robots triggered several social and ethical issues on the trust and emotional efficiency over mechanical responses. Mixed sentiments had also cropped-up among employees at the client sites in the context of human emotions, perceptions, and ethical considerations over the pre-programmed AI-driven robotic operations. The company had addressed these issues using ***emphasized and neutralized approach*** to foster relationship prior to deployments as ***meet-and-greet*** sessions. Overall, the experience of Cobalt robots is a synchronization of human-AI adaptation to emerging technology-led business modeling to offer better services at a lower price with comprehensive information analytics in real time.

References

Artz, M., & Ren, Y. (2025). Beyond the GenAI gold rush: Mapping entrepreneurial tensions in the age of generative artificial intelligence. *Annals of Anthropological Practice, 49*. https://doi.org/10.1111/napa.70016

Babushkina, D., & Votsis, A. (2022). Disruption, technology and the question of (artificial) identity. *AI and Ethics, 2*, 611–622.

Battisti, S. (2019). Digital social entrepreneurs as bridges in public–private partnerships. *Journal of Social Entrepreneurship, 10*(2), 135–158.

Berglund, H., Bousfiha, M., & Mansoori, Y. (2020). Opportunities as artifacts and entrepreneurship as design. *Academy of Management Review, 45*(4), 825–846.

Brown, S. (2024, January 17). *How generative AI is changing entrepreneurship.* Ideas made to matter. Cambridge, MIT Sloan Business School. https://mitsloan.mit.edu/ideas-made-to-matter/how-generative-ai-changing-entrepreneurship

Buhalis, D., Harwood, T., Bogicevic, V., Viglia, G., Beldona, S., & Hofacker, C. (2019). Technological disruptions in services: Lessons from tourism and hospitality. *Journal of Service Management, 30*(4), 484–506.

Cabrera, D., Colosi, L., & Lobdell, C. (2008). Systems thinking. *Evaluation and Program Planning, 31*(3), 299–310.

Carlsen, H., Dreborg, K. H., Godman, M., Hansson, S. O., Johansson, L., & Wikman-Svahn, P. (2010). Assessing socially disruptive technological change. *Technology in Society, 32*, 209–218.

Chalmers, D., MacKenzie, N. G., & Carter, S. (2021). Artificial intelligence and entrepreneurship: implications for venture creation in the fourth industrial revolution. *Entrepreneurship Theory and Practice, 45*(5), 1028–1053.

Chou, C. C. (2018). Applying design thinking method to social entrepreneurship project. *Computer Standards & Interfaces, 55*, 73–79. https://doi.org/10.1016/j.csi.2017.05.001

Fedorenko, I., Berthon, P., & Rabinovich, T. (2017). Crowded identity: Managing crowdsourcing initiatives to maximize value for participants through identity creation. *Business Horizons, 60*(2), 155–165.

Fletcher, S. R., Johnson, T. L., & Larreina, J. (2019). Putting people and robots together in manufacturing: Are we ready? In *Robotics and Well-Being* (pp. 135–147). *Springer*.

Fountaine, T., McCarthy, B., & Saleh, T. (2021, April). *Getting AI to scale*. Harvard Business Review, 1–12.

Frick, N. R., Mirbabaie, M., Stieglitz, S., & Salomon, J. (2021). Maneuvering through the stormy seas of digital transformation: The impact of empowering leadership on the AI readiness of enterprises. *Journal of Decision Systems, 30*(2–3), 235–258.

George, A. J., Rajkumar, E., John, R., Lakshmi, R., & Wajid, M. (2021). Mindfulness-based eudaimonic enhancement for well-being of individuals with alcohol-dependence: A pilot randomized controlled study. *The Open Psychology Journal, 14*(1), 167–178.

Gobble, M. M. (2016). Defining disruptive innovation. *Research-Technology Management, 59*(4), 66–71.

Gualtieri, L., Fraboni, F., De Marchi, M., & Rauch, E. (2022). Development and evaluation of design guidelines for cognitive ergonomics in human-robot collaborative assembly systems. *Applied Ergonomics, 104*. https://doi.org/10.1016/j.apergo.2022.103807

Hakim, M. P., Libera, V. M. D., Zanetta, L. D., Nascimento, L. G. P., & da Cunha, D. T. (2022). What is a dark kitchen? A study of consumer's perceptions of deliver-only restaurants using food delivery apps in Brazil. *Food Research International, 161*. https://doi.org/10.1016/j.foodres.2022.111768

Haleem, A., Javaid, M., Qadri, M. A., Singh, R. P., & Suman, R. (2022). Artificial intelligence (AI) applications for marketing: A literature-based study. *International Journal of Intelligent Networks, 3*, 119–132.

Handke, L., Aldana, A., Costa, P. L., & O'Neill, T. A. (2024). Hybrid teamwork: What we know and where we can go from here. *Small Group Research, 55*(5), 805–835.

Hopf, K., Nahr, N., Staake, T., & Lehner, F. (2024). The group mind of hybrid teams with humans and intelligent agents in knowledge-intense work. *Journal of Information Technology, 40*(1), 9–34.

Jörling, M., Böhm, R., & Paluch, S. (2019). Service robots: Drivers perceived responsibility for service outcomes. *Journal of Service Research, 22*(4), 404–420.

Khanra, S., Dhir, A., Islam, N., & Mäntymäki, M. (2020). Big data analytics in healthcare: A systematic literature review. *Enterprise Information Systems, 14*(7), 878–912.

Kolbeinsson, A., Lagerstedt, E., & Lindblom, J. (2019). Foundation for a classification of collaboration levels for human-robot cooperation in manufacturing. *Production and Manufacturing Research, 7*(1), 448–471.

Kraus, S., McDowell, W., Ribeiro-Soriano, D. E., & Rodríguez-García, M. (2021). The role of innovation and knowledge for entrepreneurship and regional development. *Entrepreneurship & Regional Development: An International Journal, 33*(3–4), 175–184.

Linnéusson, G., Boldt, S., & Rösiö, C. (2025). Investigating integration barriers and enablers in managing product platforming by using systems thinking. *Heliyon, 11*(11). https://doi.org/10.1016/j.heliyon.2025.e43472

Liu, H. Y., Maas, M., Danaher, J., Scarcella, L., Lexer, M., & Van Rompaey, L. (2020). Artificial intelligence and legal disruption: A new model for analysis. *Law, Innovation and Technology, 12*(2), 205–258. https://doi.org/10.1080/17579961.2020.1815402

Liu, Y. (2020). The micro-foundations of global business incubation: Stakeholder engagement and strategic entrepreneurial partnerships. *Technological Forecasting and Social Change, 161.* https://doi.org/10.1016/j.techfore.2020.120294

Neumeyer, X., & Santos, S. C. (2018). Sustainable business models, venture typologies, and entrepreneurial ecosystems: A social network perspective. *Journal of Cleaner Production, 172*, 4565–4579.

PWC. (2025, January 23). *Unlocking AI's potential in asset and wealth management: three actions you can take now*. Insight. Retrieved August 27, 2025, from https://www.pwc.com/us/en/industries/financial-services/library/ai-potential-asset-and-wealth-management.html

Qudrat-Ullah, H. (2025). Integrating systems thinking and AI. In *Navigating Complexity*. Springer. https://doi.org/10.1007/978-3-031-82742-6_3

Rajagopal. (2019). *Contemporary marketing strategy: Analyzing consumer behavior to drive managerial decision making*. Springer.

Rajagopal. (2021). *Sustainable businesses in developing economies - Socio-economic and governance perspectives*. Springer.

Rajagopal. (2024). *Proximity marketing: Converging community, consciousness, and consumption*. Business Exprert Press.

Rajagopal. (2025). *Virtual engagement: Managing seamless marketing with technology*. Business Expert Press.

Rajagopal, A. (2023). *Towards cleaner entrepreneurship: Bridging social consciousness and sustainability*. Palgrave Macmillan.

Raman, R., Alka, T. A., Suresh, M., & Nedungadi, P. (2025). Social entrepreneurship and sustainable technologies: Impact on communities, social innovation, and inclusive development. *Sustainable Technology and Entrepreneurship, 4*(3). https://doi.org/10.1016/j.stae.2025.100110

Rayport, J., Keller, N. T., & Park, K. K. (2023). *Cobalt robotics: Scaling workplace robotics*. Harvard Business School Publication.

Richert, A., Müller, S., Schröder, S., & Jeschke, S. (2018). Anthropomorphism in social robotics: Empirical results on human–robot interaction in hybrid production workplaces. *AI Society, 33*(3), 413–424.

Schot, J., & Steinmueller, W. E. (2018). Three frames for innovation policy: R&D, systems of innovation and transformative change. *Research Policy, 47*, 1554–1567.

Shafiabady, N., Hadjinicolaou, N., Hettikankanamage, N., Savadkoohi, E. M., Wu, R. M. X., & Vakilian, J. (2024). Explainable artificial intelligence (XAI) for improving organisational regility. *PLoS One, 19*. https://doi.org/10.1371/journal.pone.0301429

Shepherd, D., & Gruber, M. (2021). The lean startup framework: Closing the academic–practitioner divide. *Entrepreneurship Theory and Practice, 45*(5), 967–998.

Tobón, S., & Luna-Nemecio, J. (2021). Complex thinking and sustainable social development: Validity and reliability of the complex-21 scale. *Sustainability, 13*(12), 6591.

von Krogh, G. (2018). Artificial intelligence in organizations: New opportunities for phenomenon-based theorizing. *Academy of Management Discoveries, 4*(4), 404–409.

Wang, Y., & Su, X. (2021). Driving factors of digital transformation for manufacturing enterprises: A multi-case study from China. *International Journal of Technology Management, 87*(2–4), 229–253.

Wilson, J. H., & Daugherty, P. (2018, June). *Collaborative intelligence: Humans and AI are joining forces.* Harvard Business Review, 1–12.

Additional Reference

Jussupow, E., Spohrer, K., Heinzl, A., & Gawlitza, J. (2021). Augmenting medical diagnosis decisions? An investigation into physicians' decision-making process with artificial intelligence. *Information Systems Research, 32*(3), 713–735.

Kim, R. Y. (2024). The fifth wave: The sustainability age and new industrial revolution. *IEEE Engineering Management Review*, 1–12. https://doi.org/10.1109/EMR.2024.3379036

Scheibehenne, B., Greifeneder, R., & Todd, P. M. (2010). Can there ever be too many options? A meta-analytic review of choice overload. *Journal of Consumer Research, 37*(3), 409–425.

Stokel-Walker, C., & Van Noorden, R. (2023). What ChatGPT and generative AI mean for science. *Nature, 614*, 214–216.

Sturm, T., Pumplun, L., Gerlach, J. P., Kowalczyk, M., & Buxmann, P. (2023). Machine learning advice in managerial decision-making: The overlooked role of decision makers' advice utilization. *The Journal of Strategic Information Systems, 32*(4). https://doi.org/10.1016/j.jsis.2023.101790

PART II

AI and Entrepreneurship

CHAPTER 4

AI at the Grassroots

The Fifth Wave

The *Fifth Wave* of technology is a convergence of Artificial Intelligence (AI), Internet of Things (IoT), and 5G networks, which enable cloud information repositories and broadband connectivity, and encourage co-intelligence across entrepreneurship, lifestyle and values, and sustainability. Such synergy of technology fosters competitive innovation and social well-being, and helps in managing multi-tasking by integrating a wide range of datasets connecting with IoT and AI-driven machine learning (ML) to facilitate real-time decision making. This technological wave has significantly supported technology-driven entrepreneurships at the grassroots, which are identified as micro technology start-ups operating independently in the competitive marketplace and providing feeder technology support to medium- and large-scale industries, besides various service enterprises like healthcare and education (Ren et al., 2021). In addition, Fifth Wave technology supports the seamless growth of smart cities, industrial performance, and self-service technologies for quicker disposal of tasks with high-speed communication through fifth generation information and communication technology. The co-intelligence emerging as an interface of AI and human cognition has driven neural networks that enable systems to learn from real-time data, derive predictions, and

Rajagopal, A. Rajagopal, *Artificial Intelligence and Entrepreneurship*, Palgrave Studies of Entrepreneurship and Social Challenges in Developing Economies,
https://doi.org/10.1007/978-3-032-14904-6_4

automate complex tasks through IoT and hybrid modes. Entrepreneurship and AI have significantly contributed to social entrepreneurship as sustainable development by reforming and managing the existing entrepreneurial models in micro, small, and medium enterprises with increasing dependency on IoT and 5G communication (Urbano et al., 2019). AI and ML have driven the customer design thinking and relationship management to support instance-based learning and develop appropriate decision tree to build strategies and their effective implementation. The AI, ML, and IoT help in developing neural networks to enhance entrepreneurial performance through data integration and multi-layered task management (Elfatih et al., 2022).

Diverse digital technologies supported by information and communication technology and AI have modified critical entrepreneurial functions and significantly affected essential operations, processes, design thinking, new product development, and services. Digital transformation as a co-intelligence process integrates AI and human interface to disseminate communication and decision making to improve entrepreneurial competitiveness (Appio et al., 2021). AI-driven entrepreneurship has impacted deep-seated changes at multiple levels of entrepreneurial operations through AI agents in innovating and transforming new opportunities within the co-intelligence ecosystem. Accordingly, AI at the grassroots harnesses both the transformative and disruptive technologies to enhance entrepreneurial competitiveness and connect social well-being with entrepreneurial business. Interlinking entrepreneurship and technology, the concept of *Society 5.0* has outgrown as super-smart society driven by AI-led entrepreneurial paradigm to achieve technology-related competitive advantages. Consequently, the notion of *Society 5.0*, ***Entrepreneurship 5.0***, and ***Industry 5.0*** converges with the AI, ML, and the co-intelligence foundation, which responds to new business opportunities and develops influential relationships across the domains, and enables prioritizing decision-making process (Jafari-Sadeghi et al., 2021).

Entrepreneurship 5.0 focuses on resilience, sustainability, social development, and human centricity as key components of technology-led business development and manages value-creation systems to achieve socio-economic goals and become a resilient provider of holistic prosperity. As technology is an integral part of entrepreneurship, the co-existence of entrepreneurial support as feeder resource to large industries and society reinforces the use of AI and ML for the advancement of entrepreneurial activities (Maddikunta et al., 2021). Entrepreneurship 5.0 requires balancing technology adoption and decision making to develop relationship between technology and generic knowledge derived from experience and technology-mediated relationship between entrepreneurial business and society. Such combination of relationships is founded on data, information, and knowledge to drive people-centric innovation and develop interactive process cycles in cyber-physical space (Deguchi et al., 2018). This notion emphasizes the need for business analytics on real-time data that enables meaningful decision making to manage the dynamics of technology, innovation, and market. The technology-based entrepreneurship that functions on digital platforms with digital infrastructure and services can easily adapt to AI, robotics, Internet of Things (IoT), and blockchain systems to support process automation and social robotics for value creation (Çipi et al., 2023).

The early-stage ventures in local entrepreneurial ecosystem foster AI-driven design thinking, frugal innovation, and business modeling by adopting gradual digital transformation of the entrepreneurial processes for driving business growth and enhanced competitiveness. Overriding the conventional wisdom with AI poses challenges and uncertainty in decision making due to variabilities in agreements and disagreements on AI-based information. Consequently, the start-up entrepreneurship requires strategic guidance on the use of AI and ML to make appropriate decisions on manufacturing, operations in blockchain management, and continuing with the frugal innovation process (Liu et al., 2023). Though AI influences innovation and entrepreneurial activities, the acceptance of AI guidance appears to be a major challenge due to cost-time-risk (CTR) factors to ensure the effectiveness of the cost of capital, breakeven in entrepreneurial business, and strategic performance. The AI-based start-up enterprises tend to explore new opportunities, manage low-risk financial processes, and develop tactical vision on innovation, process, and market adaptability. Consequently, in the race to gain quick market share and profit, start-up enterprises often succumb to financial crunch despite the depth and speed of technological adaptation to innovation and competitive business models (BMs; Lerner & Nanda, 2023).

Artificial Intelligence is transforming all sectors of entrepreneurial trade through automation and low-frequency robots. However, automation in entrepreneurial traits has faced severe social reactions flagging the fear of human replacement. The ethical norms for the use of AI in entrepreneurial processes are yet to be defined besides the CTR factors and short-term productivity gains. It has been experienced in large companies that the use of AI has exhibited performance improvements in collaboration with human and smart machines working together. Such AI-human interface improves the symbiotic strengths of entrepreneurs, employees, and Artificial Intelligence. To achieve such convergence, AI agents need to be trained with focus on desired outputs and ensure its responsible use to improve entrepreneurial performance (Wilson & Daugherty, 2018). AI agents in turn help entrepreneurial teams with information pooling, data analytics (DA), managing repetitive tasks, customer services, and conducting physical tasks. The use of AI in entrepreneurial processes is expected to liberate entrepreneurs from routine task management and focus on creative thinking, judgment, leadership, and improving human-technology skills. Consequently, in optimizing AI output, entrepreneurs need to redesign their business models and project planning with operational flexibility. In complex projects, entrepreneurs can rely on AI to manage the work breakdown structure (WBS) by decomposing the hierarchical workflow and ensure deliverables without project scope-creep. AI also contributes substantially to project visualization by developing project charter blueprint and hierarchical task flows to enable entrepreneurs in project planning, execution, and control (Rajagopal, 2016). Entrepreneurs can also upscale projects and develop customized solutions to feed large industries and develop strategic alliances with effective human-machine interface. The attributes of AI and human interface interconnecting entrepreneurial business activities and processes have been exhibited in Figure 4.1.

Most enterprises at the grassroots are fascinated to use AI but are unable to realize the full potential of AI as they focus on applying it discretely. Consequently, AI delivers only incremental changes, which are largely tactical while the entrepreneurs fail to use the full AI potential for strategic changes that contribute to scaling up the entrepreneurial business. It is necessary to restructure entrepreneurial business models to gain full advantage of AI engaging in automation in reducing the CTR factors in business operations at the bottom line (Amoako et al., 2021). A systematic approach to engage AI to its full potential requires it to develop a comprehensive blueprint of activities and engage AI in multiple interconnected activities by visualizing data outcomes and task priorities to provide desired benefits. Aligning with AI initiatives and entrepreneurial mindset is often complex as entrepreneurial thinking and the breadth of AI information often fail to synchronize in making appropriate decisions. Therefore, categorical blueprints with hierarchical task flow across domains and subdomains could be the best fit to exploit AI to its fullest potential

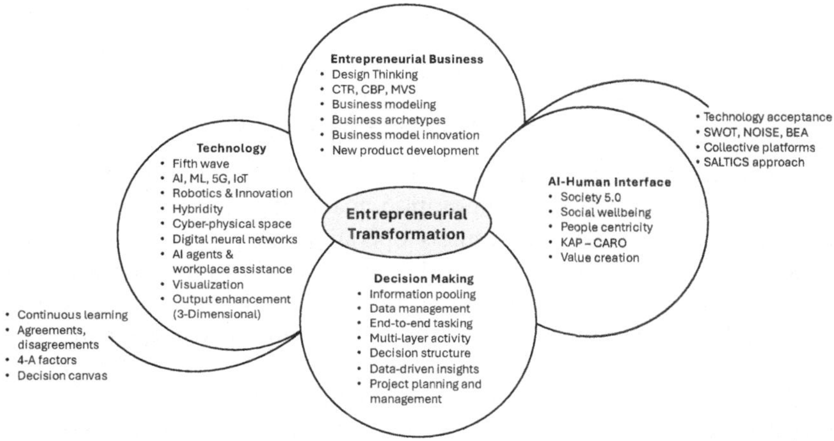

Fig. 4.1 AI and entrepreneurial transformation. (Source: Authors)

(Boateng et al., 2024). Accordingly, entrepreneurs can develop the broad workflow domains, for example, design thinking, procurement, manufacturing, supply chain, packaging, logistics and inventory, network planning, forward linkages, and end-user delivery. But commonly, entrepreneurs desiring quick outcome tend to use AI support domain-by-domain instead of applying AI unilaterally across the domains at the same time, which prolongs time, effort, and cost causing delays in decision making (Fountain et al., 2021). The potential impact of AI should be large enough to significantly improve the entrepreneurial bottom-line task and provide end-to-end efficiency in designing, developing, and delivering the tasks.

By using AI, simultaneous analysis of information across domains and subdomains can recalibrate the latent problems of enterprises such as high variability in cost and demand and streamline opportunities enabling improvements in entrepreneurial performance. The high variability is observed largely in consumer preferences, market trends, customer satisfaction, and pricing, which can be tracked using AI, and real-time decisions can be made to increase the speed of delivery and reduce the latent risks. Using AI in such complex situations is more promising than drafting employees across the domains and subdomains of entrepreneurial projects, as it is difficult to resolve the business complexities in real time using only human capital. AI provides reusable technology and data, which can be used in scenario precedences and improve project efficiency by reducing the CTR factors (Pineda, 2024).

AI-Based Business Modeling

In AI-based business model, core functions of an enterprise including manufacturing, supply chain, innovation, marketing, and sustainability are integrated to improve the business operations and deliver customized value propositions to stakeholders. The real-time decisions are supported by AI-powered analytics, automation to increase efficiency, monitor outcome and conflicts, and streamline the end-to-end task management. The major attributes of AI-based business model include mapping of co-intelligence, contextual and real-time reinforcement of critical variables, monitoring scalability of business, and integrating business ecosystem within the business models. To increase operational efficiency and reduce the CTR factors, AI-based business models focus on automation of tasks supported by the data-driven insights in decision making to develop competitive marketing, supply chain, communication, delivery, and customer relations to create value. Leveraging AI for design thinking and new product development, and in the delivery of products and services, entrepreneurs can create innovative process management and delivery systems to gain competitive advantage. However, most micro, small, and medium enterprises are struggling to realize the full potential of AI to transform their business holistically. Such complexity often arises due to discrete uses of AI without proper synchronization to the entrepreneurial needs, which causes disagreements on AI-based suggestions and automated functions. It is necessary to identify the specific area in business where AI can make significant difference over the conventional practices and manage multiple interconnected activities by sharing technology to explore competitive business opportunities (Fountain et al., 2021).

A major challenge in adapting to Artificial Intelligence in the business ecosystem is to understand organizational and cultural barriers, which often raise disagreements with AI initiatives and synchronize them within the workplace environment. This indicates that entrepreneurial co-workers, including employees and stakeholders, are struggling with the traditional mindset and are unable to accept the AI decisions that are flexible and competitively advantageous. To overcome such organizational conflicts with AI, leaders must set up AI projects with human interface where collective intelligence and co-intelligence should evolve within the technology ecosystem and orient themselves in attaining technology education and adoption of AI as an innovative agent. Accordingly, entrepreneurs can witness the AI maturity, business complexities, and the need for real-time innovation by bridging the gap between conventional entrepreneurial processes and advanced marketing needs (Fountaine et al., 2019). The common AI-based business models and archetypes include differential strategies like *enhancer, adapter, reinventor, orchestrator, and AI agent as a surface*. The *enhancer strategy* focuses on improving the operational efficiency of an enterprise with minimal disruption to existing practices with an objective to contribute to profit by reducing the CTR factors, while the *adapter strategy* enables modernization of business processes and operations by incorporating the AI and co-intelligence modules within the technology ecosystem of an enterprise. The *reinventor strategy* creates AI-driven value propositions integrating business opportunities in a holistic model, which can be orchestrated across enterprise-wide platforms for specific activities by utilizing AI and related technology tools like augmented reality (AR), virtual reality (VR), mixed reality (MR), and metaverse to project hybridity in business. With various technology tools and AI as a principal domain, the cohort of technology providers in the public domain like Google and Facebook rely on AI for transformation of processes and scaling up of business amidst traditional operating constraints. The AI-driven processes can be scaled up rapidly by connecting with inter- and intra-entrepreneurial systems to explore new opportunities by overtaking the conventional practices. Accordingly, the AI business models refined the lines between industries, enterprises, and strategies by reinforcing technological differentiations with higher implications on cost, time, risk, quality, and branding (Iansiti & Karim, 2020).

AI contributes to transforming entrepreneurial activities and processes by integrating technology and elements of entrepreneurial business by enabling effective decision making through AI-human interface as exhibited in Figure 4.1. Technology plays a significant role in transforming entrepreneurial activities and processes with the latest generation attributes, which can be identified as *Fifth Wave* comprising AI, ML, fifth-generation information and communication technology (5G-ICT), and IoT. The Fifth Wave technologies have introduced robotics in entrepreneurial activities, which significantly supported innovations by reducing the cost, time, and risk factors and enabling market-driven product designs to gain competitive advantage. By synchronizing the gap in cyber-physical activities, the *Fifth Wave* technologies could develop hybridity in managing multi-layer tasks through AI agents. In addition, digital neural networks connected through IoT have improved visualization of entrepreneurial activities and processes through three-dimensional (3-D) output enhancement by integrating real-time data (Y-axis) analytics, factors of business ecosystem (X-axis), and synchronous decision support (Z-axis). The above attributes of technology support entrepreneurial business activities and processes through precision-guided design thinking to enable new product development to meet market demand. AI commonly guides the technology-supported business archetypes to mark differential advantages through *enhancer, adapter, reinventor, orchestrator, and AI agent as a surface* strategies. Such differential approaches help in reducing the CTR factors, optimizing capital-benefit-performance (CBP) factors, and determining minimum viable segment (MVS). Consequently, *Fifth Wave* technologies help entrepreneurs in technology-based business modeling and improve business models periodically through process innovations.

Decision making and AI-human interface have outgrown from the integration of technology with entrepreneurial activities and processes in business. Decision-making process among entrepreneurs is highly benefited from the adaptation of technology and AI tools to analyze complex scenarios by pooling information, data management, and streamlining end-to-end task performance. The technology-based decision-making platforms enable entrepreneurs to conduct multi-layer activities. The use of AI tools categorically supports short-term and long-term decision structures on simple and complex business scenarios by analyzing various functional factors like procurement, supply chain, manufacturing, processing, marketing, and value creation through data-driven insights. Technology and AI support help entrepreneurs in project planning with precision by analyzing the SIPOC elements comprising supply, inputs, process, outputs, and customers besides the foundation of the entrepreneurial projects determined by analyzing DMAIC factors (define, measure, analyze, innovate/implement, and control).

By streamlining technology, elements of entrepreneurial business, and decision making, the AI-human interface significantly creates value in revolutionizing Society 5.0, and social well-being through knowledge-adaptability-practices (KAP) driven by consistency-accuracy-reliability-output expectation (CARO). The AI-human interface grows with people's centricity and generates enormous co-intelligence blending AI inputs with personalized knowledge and experience. The convergence of technology and decision tools requires continuous learning to match the speed of technology and changing dynamics of business scenarios. Accordingly, entrepreneurs match their co-intelligence to perceive agreements and disagreements on AI-based suggestions and activity maps. Broadly, the 4-A factors comprising awareness (changing technology), attributes (elements supporting entrepreneurial scenarios), adaptability (CTR and CBP factors), and affordability (entrepreneurial economics of technology) determine various elements of decision canvas leading to entrepreneurial actions and performance.

Making entrepreneurial decisions in the changing entrepreneurial business scenarios and the increasing need of AI-human interface are critical to technology acceptance in the context of entrepreneurial economics and business growth. These factors require comprehensive analysis of strength, weakness, opportunities, and threats (SWOT) combined with the analysis of needs, opportunities, innovation, strengths, and expectations (NOISE) factors and breakeven analysis (BEA) considering the embedded risk in entrepreneurial activities. In developing economies, the *Fifth Wave* technological tools can be adapted by the entrepreneurs on collective platforms through SALTICS approaches comprising *sharing, analyzing, learning, transforming, co-intelligence,* and *sustainability*, which enables technology to benefit entrepreneurial communities.

Artificial Intelligence (AI)-driven business model innovation (BMI) has experienced a recent surge in business practices with high impact on industries. However, this outgrowth of technology remains fragmented due to the business complexities and discrete information analysis. Predominantly micro, small, and medium enterprises are transforming their business models despite lack of resources and skills that emphasize acquainting with the technological aspects of AI implementation in business models (BMs), treating BMI as an essential growth requirement in dynamic marketplace. Additionally, the public-private partnership, government programs, and large industry's corporate social responsibility toward micro, small, and medium enterprises have laid significant emphasis on the use of AI in BMI to make the entrepreneurial segment stronger and competitive. Consequently, the recent attention of entrepreneurs is toward experimenting with generative AI and chatbots for quick acquisition of information and gaining guidance on disruptive innovation (Burger et al., 2023). As a result, a large number of enterprises at the grassroots are engaging with AI and technology platforms in managing business model innovation by demonstrating data-driven decision making in a real-time application with added accuracy and reliability of AI. Besides upscaling manufacturing, supply chain, and delivery systems, most companies have also achieved efficiency in customer services across multiple channels by integrating AI-driven data analysis into business modeling to generate customized effects on products and services (Burström et al., 2021).

It has been observed by business executives and entrepreneurs that AI allows firms to maintain and gain competitive advantages while most executives believe that AI enables creating opportunities for new business models by leveraging value creation and developing new capabilities to manage BMI for competitive advantage (Foss & Saebi, 2017). Broadly, AI is considered an umbrella for use of different tools associated with machine learning (ML), which is a collection of mathematical models or algorithms that independently improve database decision making under ***supervised, unsupervised, or reinforced learning***. A ***supervised learning*** systematically arranges algorithms and trains the algorithmic process by labeling data to identify point-to-point connections (service provider to end user) displaying input and output data with minimum and maximum limits (Eling et al., 2022). Deep learning (DL) has gained widespread attention in changing technological ecosystems as a tool of architecture of entrepreneurial mindset in the process of BMI. Deep learning tries to process large volume of data through artificial neural networks to classify the data and help in categorical decision making (Mishra & Tripathi, 2021).

Data Analytics and Deep Learning

Data analytics (DA) and deep learning (DL) are symbiotic and connected with AI and ML applications, which enable entrepreneurs in design thinking and process streamlining to create end-user value. Deep learning has one of the active ML outcomes contributing to numerous scientific and technological platforms including task processes, design thinking, real-time data analytics, and other relevant business information. Data analytics in entrepreneurship has emerged as an essential tool for decision making where raw data is often unfiltered, unlabeled, and uncategorized. The AI-supported DA and DL techniques contribute to the contemporary state-of-the-art management of entrepreneurial tasks and business modeling synchronizing with the IoT data accreditations to resolve various complexities and challenges including the management of CTR factors. Real-time data-intensive applications help entrepreneurs to manage DL processes by analyzing various entrepreneurial project management streams. AI helps in streamlining DMAIC that comprises defining entrepreneurial needs, developing task-based *measures*, *analyzing* real-time data related to market and consumer behavior, determining *implementation* process and stages, and exercising key process *controls* in entrepreneurial task management. The effective use of AI along with DA and DL helps entrepreneurs in identifying quality function deployment (QFD) based on identifying needs, opportunities, innovation, strengths, and expectations (NOISE) by understanding the voice-of-customers (VoC). In the entrepreneurial projects of innovative product development to gain competitive advantage, it is necessary to analyze VoC to manage appropriate QFD, which supports the entrepreneurial business process contextual to NOISE determinants. AI also helps in analyzing data-text-mining information to derive global perspectives on key entrepreneurial activities and synchronize them with VoC. AI also enables the manufacturing-to-market task flows within the business canvas comprising the following elements (Rajagopal, 2025):

- Key activities: comprise understanding consumer behavior and analyzing market trends to develop appropriate designs and manage business operations to deliver products/services to end users.
- Key partners: uncover meaningful partners and analyze useful information on business operations and streamline the entrepreneurial process using AI and ML support.
- Key resources: include analyzing CTR factors, cost-to-capital, break-even analysis, and performance management through key performance indicators within global and minimum viable segments.
- Value proposition: value streams by entrepreneurial activities need to be determined by identifying the start and finish points to create value in diverse activities using advanced analytics specifically based on AI, ML, and DL techniques.
- Customer relationships: AI and ML are contemporary tools to analyze consumer behavior and practice customer relationship management with meaningful insights and gain trust by developing self-service technology options to resolve basic issues and increase the speed of service. Entrepreneurs can improve DL experience using AI to explore consumer complexities, create *awareness*, develop appropriate *attributes*, provide *comprehensive* information, and map required *action* points to improve customer relationships and services.
- Channels: AI and ML enable omnichannel strategy to improve entrepreneurial business performance. Entrepreneurs can evaluate

the channel's performance through data analytics, visualization, and measuring channel metrics.

- Customer segmentation: analyzing geo-demographic data entrepreneurs can identify consumer segments by analyzing qualitative (trend, quality, preferences, self-actualization, psychodynamics, and social value and lifestyle) and quantitative (CTR, price, and promotion) data points.
- Cost structure: real-time cost comparison in manufacturing and operational processes can be supported by using AI in data-text-mining and data visualization to gain a competitive map of cost structure.
- Revenue streams: AI also enables entrepreneurs to identify alternate revenue streams within the area of entrepreneurial expertise to develop new activities and target the existing market segment. Alternatively, entrepreneurs can also identify new entrepreneurial activity with new business models to target new geo-demographic market segments to secure alternate revenue streams while strengthening the principal revenue stream.

Deep learning is a specialized field of AI and ML, which uses multi-layered neural networks to enable comprehensive learning and analyzing complex patterns in real-time data-based decision making. Accordingly, DL enables contemporary learning experience and multi-layer information processing using verbal and non-verbal data. In this process, AI helps in object recognition, speech clarification, data visualization, and language translation with high accuracy. DL has benefited by the advanced AI systems built on large language models (LLM) and autonomous content analysis and data driving technology (Selmy et al., 2024).

Synchronizing data analytics and deep learning improves the decision-making abilities in enterprises of different sizes and scales of operations. Deep learning enhances the decision-making process by simplifying complex scenarios and connecting with real-time data to identify possible entrepreneurial processes and operational patterns aligning with the industrial and market ecosystems. Comprehensive data analytics helps entrepreneurs to understand the current manufacturing and market trends and enable them to explore new opportunities through AI-based precision forecasting to measure financial trends, market demand, trend-based designing, and contemporary practices and organizational manuscript. Deep learning enhances decision making by recognizing advanced patterns and managing unstructured data like images, text, and sensor readings through AI support. Entrepreneurs are able to learn from chronological data on demand, financial analysis, and marketing-mix attributes to generate accurate predictions for business growth. By processing large volumes of information, AI-driven deep learning augments decision-making capabilities among entrepreneurs to derive robust insights and creative measures (Wang et al., 2025). Automated data processing and outcome analysis enable entrepreneurs to make appropriate decisions in their business projects, streamlining the project charter and work breakdown structure from initial activity to the end of project activities. Accordingly, data analytics and deep learning have symbiotic effects, which strengthen each stage of the decision-making process on decision canvas as exhibited in Figure 4.2.

The decision canvas has a linear path to decision outcomes, which is spread across seven stages in entrepreneurial activities. In the complex business scenarios, it is necessary for the entrepreneurs to precisely determine the problem, target, and required analysis (PTA) in the process of developing right decision. Identifying PTA lays the foundation in the decision-making process and sets the layers of influencing elements while eliminating the intervening elements. By ascertaining what needs to be decided, entrepreneurs must identify values and rationale associated with

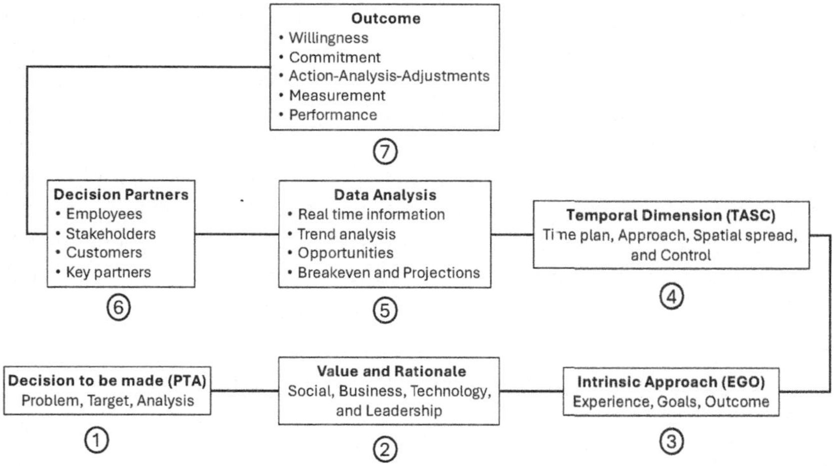

Fig. 4.2 Decision canvas. (Source: Authors)

the decision-making process. Accordingly, the values associated with social well-being, business process, technology adaptation, and leadership needs must be identified to support the decision-making process. Decision leadership is commonly affected by self-esteem and experience of entrepreneurs. Therefore, it is necessary for entrepreneurs to rely on data analytics and deep learning to enable self-actualization, which helps in defining intrinsic approaches based on entrepreneurial *experience*, entrepreneurial *goals*, and expected *outcome* (EGO). Entrepreneurial cognition, KAP, and CARO factors significantly support the EGO elements in decision making, which categorically align with the project charter and work breakdown structure (WBS) of entrepreneurial projects. The decision on WBS can be spread across *time* plans, activity *approaches*, *spatial spread*, and *control* measures (TASC), which are often complex, and incorrect or overriding decisions may cause cost creep that affects the CTR factors and deliverables at the end of the entrepreneurial project. However, accuracy in data analysis based on real-time information, trend analysis, and breakeven and projection modeling significantly affects the TASC factors to take appropriate decisions based on PTA considerations. The AI and technology-based decision platforms help entrepreneurs in integrating various business players into decision making by sharing the process on the decision canvas. The broad decision partners include employees, stakeholders, customers, and key partners, engaged in supply chain and strategic alliances in overall entrepreneurial activities. By conducting decision-making processes through the stages described above, entrepreneurs can expect the decision outcome, which requires both tangible and intangible endorsements. Consequently, the emerging outcomes of the decision process need to ensure the willingness toward accepting the decision, developing commitment, and leading to proper implementation. The agreeable decision can be subjected to categorical *action*, periodical *analysis*, and scenario *adjustments* (A-3 factors), and appropriate measures to evaluate the implementation at various stages need to be developed. Finally, the entrepreneurs will be able to measure the performance of the project charter in the context of the decision outcome derived through the decision canvas.

Immersive Business and Real-Time Decisions

Immersive business technology is built around augmented reality (AR), virtual reality (VR), and mixed reality (MR), which converges multi-sensing experiences of customers, employees, and business partners for self-actualization and deep learning within the AI and technology ecosystem. The combination of AR, VR, and MR has led to new immersive business experience and visibility in metaverse business strategy that foster deeper cognitive learning, and virtual living and being of business ecosystem in promoting brands, products, and processes by engaging active participation of business partners and customers. The key application of immersive businesses has been observed in technology start-ups and virtual business communities (e-commerce and social media business platforms) that are oriented in enhancing the boundaryless marketing and sales experiences (Fan et al., 2025). The immersive business experiences include creating virtual showrooms, interactive product visualizations, and AI-powered product demonstrations to enable customers to attain three-dimensional experience (product attributes, attractiveness, and self-esteem) to contextualize NOISE factors and make appropriate decisions. Immersive experience helps customers to retain information on products and services in memorable ways to clip it at top-of-the-mind and boost brand loyalty. Developing immersive learning experience and virtual onboarding of technology companies requires adequate training and education to key partners, customers, and employees to improve the virtual performance of visual business strategies and set them for key challenges.

The immersive business experience can be provided through virtual shared spaces remotely for customers, sales and service teams, and business partners to collaborate on new strategies and make decisions in real time by enhancing the competitive dynamics and market attractiveness. A combination of AR, VR, and MR integrating with the AI support, immersive business experience leads to establishing emotional connections of customers with brands by generating technology tags for wider cognitive analysis (Rauschnabel et al., 2019). Such interactive immersions in technology platforms often challenge customer engagements and employee follow-ups to stay onboard technology platforms. However, complex data and virtual products and services design an intricate visualization process in attaining immersive business experience. The interactive data with simple content management enables immersive environments popular by allowing inflow of customers on technology platforms. Streamlined internal processes and improved designs help virtual companies in streamlining marketing, sales, and productivity besides delivering interactive training and collaboration among various business partners. The immersive businesses not only enable firms to increase customer and employee engagement, and loyalty, but also help in developing deeper connections by fostering the sense of real and omnipresence within virtual environments. Expanding opportunities and improving operational efficiency are embedded in immersive businesses, which reduce cyber-physical gaps and restructure conventional workspaces to digital workstations significantly contributing to circular economy. Immersive business is an endorsement to forward thinking and pioneering virtual business platforms like metaverse, which demonstrates the contribution of AI and technology in fostering cyber-physical and neurobehavioral drivers in the *Fifth Wave* business ecosystem.

Most micro, small, and medium enterprises are at the edge of tradeoff between conventional practices and adapting to technological advancements by making appropriate choice of immersive technologies for promoting consumer products and services as immersive businesses also focus on immersive media for marketing. However, the underlying cognitive dilemma among entrepreneurs creates disagreements in adapting to AI-based technology platforms and immersive experiences in real time. However, the AR, VR, and MR technologies enrich entrepreneur's real-time experiences and foster appropriate decision making by integrating virtual market information, design thinking, and strategy development. This helps entrepreneurs to develop products to match with the personal surroundings of consumers and develop positive cognitive, emotional, and behavioral responses. Therefore, advertising appeals in immersive businesses look for realistic experience, decision comfort, and reduced CTR factors. The AR and VR technologies allow consumers to experience product features and embedded values as an ideal within virtual environment, which is offered by the tech-savvy firms through interactive and vivid displays that enable consumers to feel fully immersed (Wedel et al., 2020). Compared to conventional entrepreneurial models, immersive entrepreneurship with AR, VR, and MR virtual platforms provides informative, novel, and entertaining experiences to enhance consumers' perceived accuracy and authenticity of associated information to foster differential marketing strategy. The interactive website presentations along with AR and VR technology platforms stimulate the functionality of products and services, which contribute to greater novelty, immersion, cyber-physical integration, geo-demographic presence, personalization, informativeness, and enhanced-perceived usefulness. Consequently, immersive experience in entrepreneurship and business is a new state of art in design thinking, manufacturing, virtual store ergonomics, deep learning, self-actualization, and self-esteem (Uhm et al., 2022).

AI enables managers to streamline immersive and interactive experiences with consumers and business partners including supply chain players. Virtual reality (VR) technology is a promising tool for managers to create these experiences, as evidenced by the increasing and successful VR marketing applications used by the e-commerce firms. Though there are many studies published on the role of ICT and technology-led marketing applications, little guidance is available on how the advanced technological experiences in marketing can be strategically designed to create favorable customer perceptions, attitudes, and behaviors. Immersive experiences emerge largely with the digital branding approach in e-commerce firms. This includes creating a distinctive logo, engaging color palettes, and expressive typography that are consistently applied across all digital platforms by utilizing augmented reality (AR) and virtual reality (VR) to create interactive and engaging brand experiences. AR can help customers in visualizing products in their own environment and generate significant customer value (Rajagopal, 2025).

Digital firms engaged in business-to-business (B2B), business-to-consumer, and hybrid marketing develop and post compelling narratives and produce high-quality content on product websites like storyboards, blog posts, videos, and infographics to attract and engage your audience to reinforce the brands. These contents help in using consumer data to create targeted campaigns that resonate with individual preferences, enhancing customer satisfaction and loyalty. In addition, firms benefit from social media participation through active customer participation in conversations on various types of digital content, sharing views, and using collective intelligence analytics to fine-tune brand strategies. Digital brand development is also benefited by collaborating with social media influencers to reach new audiences and build credibility to brands (Rajagopal, 2025). In the United States, by contrast, though platforms such as Amazon Marketplace and eBay continue to increase their share, brand-owned and more brand-friendly online retail, including those sites with limited control, accounts for about 70% of all e-commerce (Bu, 2015).

To implement immersive technology, firms need to make efforts to understand customers' response to immersive experiences and how AR works in enhancing the impact on business. Accordingly, the aspiring firms can initiate AR-powered virtual pilot projects. However, interactive product videos are a good plan to start with to experiment with the AR effect. The e-commerce firms use live shopping platforms for real-time engagement, and these platforms enable hosting real-time product demonstrations, interactive sessions, and offer exclusive promotions. Metaverse technology is a collection of technologies that enable the creation of virtual 3D worlds where users can interact, work, learn, and more. The metaverse is a concept that refers to a collective virtual shared space created by the convergence of virtually enhanced physical and digital reality. It is often described as the next iteration of the internet, where users can be represented by avatars and interact in immersive 3D environment (Rajagopal, 2025).

Case Studies

CS1: McCormick and Company

McCormick and Company (MC) is an American company, founded in 1889 with global brand penetration in distributing spices, herbs, and other flavoring agents. The company is engaged in procuring categorical spices and distributing through retail outlets, besides manufacturing food products and extending food services in international markets. The company is known for its umbrella brand for spices, extracts, sauces, and marinates, including gourmet products. Its brand is present in over 150 countries, which sources ingredients for its spice blend products from over 75 countries. Its presence is prominent in the Latin American countries. The company faced major challenges in adapting to AI tools in developing new products with technological partnership with IBM Research during 2020. The major task was to develop interface with suppliers and product developers and manage global supply chain across cross-country locations. The underlying challenges in adapting to AI and ML include technology enhancement in new product development using AI and ML by analyzing market data, procurement data, manufacturing data, product formulas, consumer taste analysis reports, and market trends to generate a new blend of flavors and accelerate product innovation.

The AI-driven approach allows the company to develop ONE-AI platform to serve retail inventory and launch a set of single-dish recipe-mix blends and explore new business opportunities for mass customization and personalized product deliveries targeted through e-commerce. The key aspects of AI deployment of MC have raised concerns on data-driven innovation, accelerated new product development, e-commerce, and customization. The company proposed to use IBM's AI system and analyze consumer behavior and proximity to identify new consumption patterns and collect information on ingredient ratios and flavors to develop new product blends. The AI system as an enabler was expected to reduce CTR factors allowing food engineers to develop new products within the project charter. Using AI and ML tools to accelerate product development requires adequate training to employees to contribute to new product development seamlessly by optimizing the manufacturing process and synchronizing with the delivery of products to retail outlets and individuals through e-commerce. The ONE-AI enabled product platform to launch new product lines within extended product portfolios, which included new spice blends like Tuscan Chicken and Bourbon Pork Tenderloin, designed to season both protein and vegetable.

The capability of AI and ML was estimated to ride over the natural intelligence of human behavior and provide new dimensions on visual perceptions and reasoning about new products. AI was expected to provide sensory stimulus, product comprehension, and facilitate consumer learning. The goal of AI was to enable creativity by constructing a program capable of executing the design and creativity of new products, formulating appropriate algorithms to learn about consumer perceptions and design manufacturing process blueprints to optimize production. One of the major challenges in deploying AI in new product development projects of MC has been the trust in AI among product developers. The company identified the following areas, which required employees to trust AI-based analysis in decision making:

- Analysis given by AI on childhood emotions and experiences of consumers based on the data analyzed by AI.
- Suggestions from collective experiences of success and failure as analyzed by AI.
- The redundancy in AI data and the embedded biasness in the AI-suggested solutions.
- Cognitive and psychometric analysis based on data mining conducted by AI to suggest utilitarian and hedonic motivations toward acceptability of new product blends.
- To synchronize product design suggested by AI with employees' consensus and market trend.

Managing global-local dynamics in the context of local culture, consumer preferences, and crowd cognition has been difficult to validate due to data inconsistencies, biasness, and the changing consumer preferences.

Evaluating the roadmap of the company in adapting to AI and ML tools, the major challenge faced by the decision makers is about the underlying risk in agreeing with AI-based suggestions in developing new product processes, which were yet to be validated in the market. However, the company has made valid attempts to secure the buy-in of product developers alongside building with the AI system; there existed the risk of agreeing to AI suggestions without field-based analysis and managerial consensus. Overriding the conventional wisdom, the company decided to engage with AI and promote the continuous involvement of product developers by analyzing AI-based information and decision making. From the market perspective for a food company like McCormick, the global-local convergence in new product development is risky because of spatial differences in consumer preferences and adaptability to new tastes. By the end of 2020, AI was deployed as a new product development process and the market response continued to support the AI-suggested flavors despite sporadic underlying managerial disagreements.

CS2: Champo Carpets, India

Champo is an Indian manufacturer and exporter of handmade and mechanized carpets and rugs. The company has a vertically integrated production and operations system, which controls the production process through a project-planning mechanism with an appropriate work breakdown structure. The company has a standing of over five decades in manufacturing and exporting retail brands of carpets and rugs from India. It is largely an artisan-based company with a wide artisanal network that provides handmade carpets and rugs that are manufactured from sustainable natural material consisting of BCI cotton, recycled polyester, jute, and bamboo fiber. The company serves both business-to-business and business-to-consumer market segments. The company has had a complex manufacturing process of carpets as the company shared designs with potential customers to motivate purchase orders. The sample design selection was done manually, which had a long process and was expensive. In order to streamline the manufacturing process with market trends, the company visited various trade shows and shared samples with clients on trends in fiber and colors. This process did not support streamlining the CTR factors, causing an increase in the cost of manufacturing, time of delivery, and the embedded quality risks. Consequently, the company has lost several opportunities due to process mismatches and inaccurate targeting of products to identify clients. To overcome the challenge of the conventional manufacturing process, the company has implemented enterprise resource planning (ERP) application to support data analytics by recapturing data at every level of the manufacturing process, ranging from designing to delivery.

One of the major challenges in the carpet manufacturing industry is developing new designs with cost-effective manufacturing processes. Therefore, addressing the needs of customers in terms of developing new designs has emerged as a cost-intensive activity comprising raw material and dyeing costs accounting for 30% of the total cost, besides the weaving cost of 60% and finishing cost (shearing/clipping, washing/dipping, stretching, backing, etc.) of 10%. Champo Carpets Company has been vertically integrated in manufacturing and exporting carpets with focus on B2B global clientele. The company has adopted AI and ML tools in developing new designs and manufacturing process maps by realizing the data available from the ERP platform. The AI tools enable identifying potential customers and connecting new designs with them using suitable attributes from available data and an appropriate analytics model to create appropriate customer segments and a preference matrix. Accordingly, the recommendations made by AI tools help the company in developing appropriate strategies in improving the sample-to-order process with a low conversion rate yielding reduced costs for targeted products. The generative AI enabled the carpet designers to create new design patterns based on client preferences, traditional motifs, and changing market trends to gear up the manufacturing process with AI-based designs. The use of AI and ML enables decision makers to analyze real-time data, develop designs, and adjust machine settings for machine-made carpets to optimize production and reduce waste during the manufacturing process. AI tool, which translates complex designs into simplified codes reducing the weaving time in producing complex pattern carpets, has been used to assist traditional carpet weavers for weaving handmade carpets. The AI software namely Talim helped in weaving complex carpet patterns of Kashmiri tradition.

The AI-driven systems significantly contributed to identifying defects overriding human errors in weaving like discoloration, inconsistency in weaving, and fiber knots. The AI tools also ensured automated optical inspection with high-resolution cameras across the weaving looms to ensure uniform quality. In addition, AI algorithms have been useful in analyzing both the demand and sales data, social media trends, and production indicators alongside mapping the demand variation for specific colors and patterns. Such information helps decision makers to develop strategic approaches in managing inventory by avoiding overproduction and stocking of final products. For high-end hand-woven carpets, AI combined with blockchain technology helped in simplifying logistics and inventory system and also identifying the counterfeit products. By optimizing energy consumption and optimizing the usage of dye, AI has significantly contributed to the sustainability perspectives of the company.

Technology and Social Empowerment

Social empowerment of technology enables both equity and equality across the demographic sections in a society and helps them to exercise equal control over their lifestyle, income resources, and employment. Empowering society holistically drives the members to take important decisions in routine activities and creates equal social and economic opportunities to support their lifestyle and socio-economic status (Nord et al., 2016). Empowering technology in all sections of society equally ensures strong economic growth and social development in a region. On a collective level, social empowerment of technology is implemented through public policies, corporate social responsibilities delivered by the corporations, public sector organizations, and social institutions, which help members of economically marginalized social communities. The social empowerment of technology aims at improving the social and economic stature of marginalized communities including gender-based classes to improve their returns on assets, good health, education, social belonging, self-esteem, and self-confidence and develop economic opportunity. Holistically, social empowerment is developed across the four principal dimensions comprising psychological, organizational, economic, and cultural among the members of the community (Rajagopal, 2024).

Improving social quality in the context of values and lifestyle, communication, decision making, and 3Es comprising equity, equality, experience within the community entails many challenges. Often communities are built orthogonally and grow independently over time. Such communities with rigid values do not accept external influence and adapt to new environment. Such behavioral independence in the community is often challenging to introduce any alterations in the societal attributes, as understanding and influencing the social conventions, acquiring, and testing new attributes, or modifying the existing practices within the community are rigid and time consuming. Therefore, it is necessary to meticulously embed social empowerment in the community and specify its distinctiveness in relation to other theories and practices of empowerment (Rajagopal, 2024).

Benefits of social empowerment of technology can theoretically be linked to optimizing the use value of products and services from the design-to-society, design-to-market, and design-to-value perspectives (Rajagopal, 2021). In the sustainability sector, various studies on health, energy, and communication have highlighted that large-scale social marketing infrastructure for renewable energy products like solar photovoltaic panel for home lighting, appliances, and to some extent, machine functions, have made a significant dent in delivering the social and economic benefits to the stakeholders (Zang et al., 2021). Previous studies have shown that the social empowerment of women toward using the non-conventional energy for domestic use has significantly increased the use of solar cookers in the developing countries, which has consequently improved the social and economic status of women. Social empowerment builds cognitive reasoning, capabilities to develop strategy, and appropriate decision making among the consumers and stakeholders. It is crucial to the idea of coping with changing corporate strategies and managing behavioral change proneness and resistance of consumers and stakeholders (Gruss et al., 2020).

References

Amoako, G., Omari, P., Kumi, D. K., Agbemabiase, G. C., & Asamoah, G. (2021). Conceptual framework—Artificial intelligence and better entrepreneurial decision-making: the influence of customer preference, industry benchmark, and employee involvement in an emerging market. *Journal of Risk and Finance Management, 14*(12), 604.

Appio, F., Frattini, F., Petruzzelli, A., & Neirotti, P. (2021). Digital transformation and innovation management: a synthesis of existing research and an agenda for future studies. *Journal of Product Innovation Management, 38*(1), 4–20.

Boateng, S. L., Penu, O. K. A., Boateng, J. B. R., Marfo, J. S., Anning-Dorson, T., & Broni, F. E. J. (2024). Mapping the Research on Artificial Intelligence and Entrepreneurship. *International Journal of E-Entrepreneurship and Innovation, 14*(1). https://doi.org/10.4018/IJEEI.343790

Bu, L. (2015, December). Can Brands Control their Online destiny. *McKinsey Insights.* McKinsey & Co.

Burger, B., Kanbach, D. K., Kraus, S., Breier, M., & Corvello, V. (2023). On the use of AI-based tools like ChatGPT to support management research. *European Journal of Innovation Management, 26*(7), 233–241.

Burström, T., Parida, V., Lahti, T., & Wincent, J. (2021). AI-enabled business-model innovation and transformation in industrial ecosystems: A framework, model and outline for further research. *Journal of Business Research, 127*, 85–95.

Çipi, A., Fernandes, A. C. R. D., Ferreira, F. A. F., Ferreira, N. C. M. Q. F., & Meidutė-Kavaliauskienė, I. (2023). Detecting and developing new business opportunities in society 5.0 contexts: A sociotechnical approach. *Technology in Society, 73*. https://doi.org/10.1016/j.techsoc.2023.102243

Deguchi, A., Hirai, C., Matsuoka, H., Nakano, T., Oshima, K., Tai, M., & Tani, S. (2018). What is Society 5.0? In O. Kamimura (Ed.), *Society 5.0: A People-Centric Super-smart Society* (pp. 1–23). Springer Open.

Elfatih, N. M., Hasan, M. K., Kamal, Z., Gupta, D., Saeed, R. A., Ali, E. S., & Hosain, M. S. (2022). Internet of vehicle's resource management in 5G networks using AI technologies: Current status and trends. *IET Communications, 16*(5), 400–420.

Eling, M., Nuessle, D., & Staubli, J. (2022). The impact of artificial intelligence along the insurance value chain and on the insurability of risks. *The Geneva Papers on Risk and Insurance-- Issues and Practice, 47*(2), 205–241.

Fan, X., Xun, J., Dolega, L., Li, Y., & Chong, W. K. (2025). Immersive technologies in retailing: a CiteSpace bibliometric analysis. *EuroMed Journal of Business*. https://doi.org/10.1108/EMJB-04-2025-0159

Foss, N. J., & Saebi, T. (2017). Fifteen Years of Research on Business Model Innovation. *Journal of Management, 43*(1), 200–227.

Fountaine, T., McCarthy, B., & Saleh, T. (2019). Building the AI-Powered Organization: Technology Is Not the Biggest Problem. Culture is. *Harvard Business Review, 97*, 62. https://wuyuansheng.com/doc/Databricks-AI-Powered-Org__Article-Licensing-July21-1.pdf

Gruss, R., Abrahams, A., Song, Y., Berry, D., & Al-Daihani, S. M. (2020). Community building as an effective user engagement strategy: a case study in academic libraries. *Journal of Association of Information Science and Technology, 71*(2), 208–220.

Iansiti, M., & Karim, R. L. (2020). *Competing in the Age of AI: Strategy and Leadership When Algorithms and Networks Run the World*. Harvard Business Review Press.

Jafari-Sadeghi, V., Garcia-Perez, A., Candelo, E., & Couturier, J. (2021). Exploring the impact of digital transformation on technology entrepreneurship and technological market expansion: the role of technology readiness, exploration and exploitation. *Journal of Business Research, 124*, 100–111.

Lerner, J., & Nanda, R. (2023). Venture capital and innovation. In *Handbook of the Economics of Corporate Finance* (Vol. 1, pp. 77–105). North-Holland. https://doi.org/10.1016/bs.hecf.2023.02.002

Liu, L., Jiang, H., & Zhang, Y. (2023). The impact of venture capital on Chinese SMEs' sustainable development: a focus on early-stage and professional characteristics. *Humanities and Social Science Communications, 10*(1), 1–11. https://doi.org/10.1057/s41599-023-01893-7

Maddikunta, P., Pham, Q., Prabadevi, B., Deepa, N., Dev, K., Gadekallu, T., Ruby, R., & Liyanage, M. (2021). Industry 5.0: a survey on enabling technologies and potential applications. *Journal of Industrial Information Integration, 26*, 1–19.

Mishra, S., & Tripathi, A. R. (2021). AI business model: an integrative business approach. *Journal of Innovation and Entrepreneurship., 10*(1), 18–39. https://doi.org/10.1186/s13731-021-00157-5

Nord, J. H., Lee, T.-R., Çetin, F., Atay, O., & Paliszkiewicz, J. (2016). Examining the impact of social technologies on empowerment and economic development. *International Journal of Information Management, 36*(6, Part A), 1101–1110.

Pineda, M. V. B. (2024). New entrepreneurial strategies using the new technologies of artificial intelligence and NFT in the field of the music industry. *Journal of Digital Economy, 3*, 260–274.

Rajagopal. (2016). *Innovative Business Projects: Breaking Complexities, Building Performance (Vol. 1)-Fundamentals and Project Environment*. Business Expert Press.

Rajagopal. (2021). *The Business Design Cube: Converging Markets, Society, and Customer Values to Grow Competitive in Business*. Business Expert Press.

Rajagopal. (2024). *Proximity Marketing: Converging Community, Consciousness, and Consumption*. Business Expert Press.

Rajagopal. (2025a). *Contemporary Marketing Strategy: Analyzing Consumer Behavior to Drive Managerial Decision Making* (2nd ed.). Palgrave Macmillan.

Rajagopal. (2025b). *Virtual Engagement: Managing Seamless Marketing with Technology*. Business Expert Press.

Rauschnabel, P. A., Felix, R., & Hinsch, C. (2019). Augmented reality marketing: how mobile AR-apps can improve brands through inspiration. *Journal of Retailing and Consumer Services, 49*(1), 43–53.

Ren, P., Xiao, Y., Chang, X., Po-Yao, H., Li, Z., Gupta, B. B., Chen, X., & Wang, X. (2021). A survey of deep active learning. *ACM Computing Surveys (CSUR), 54*(9), 1–40.

Selmy, H. A., Mohamed, H. K., & Medhat, W. (2024). Big data analytics deep learning techniques and applications: A survey. *Information Systems, 120*. https://doi.org/10.1016/j.is.2023.102318

Uhm, J.-P., Kim, S., Do, C., & Lee, H.-W. (2022). How augmented reality (AR) experience affects purchase intention in sport E-commerce: Roles of perceived diagnosticity, psychological distance, and perceived risks. *Journal of Retailing and Consumer Services, 67.* https://doi.org/10.1016/j.jretconser.2022.103027

Urbano, D., Aparicio, S., & Audretsch, D. (2019). Twenty-five years of research on institutions, entrepreneurship, and economic growth: What has been learned? *Small Business Economics, 53*(1), 21–49.

Wang, X., Zhang, B., Xu, Z., Qin, Y., & Chen, C. L. P. (2025). An exploration of deep learning for decision making: Methods, applications, and challenges. *Expert Systems with Applications, 289.* https://doi.org/10.1016/j.eswa.2025.128406

Wedel, M., Bigné, E., & Zhang, J. (2020). Virtual and augmented reality: advancing research in consumer marketing. *International Journal of Research in Marketing, 37*(3), 443–465.

Wilson, J. H., & Daugherty, P. (2018). Collaborative Intelligence: Humans and AI Are Joining Forces. *Harvard Business Review*

Zang, D., Li, F., & Chandio, A. A. (2021). Factors of energy poverty: evidence from Tibet, China. *Sustainability, 13*(17), 1–20.

CHAPTER 5

Business Modeling

AI Infrastructure Planning

Digital infrastructure for entrepreneurship requires development of new channels that are compatible with AI-based platforms to nurture individual entrepreneurship and stimulate design thinking, precision process maps for manufacturing supply chain, inventory, logistics, marketing, and customer relationship management. Development of digital infrastructure with adaptability to Artificial Intelligence (AI) and machine learning (ML) has injected strong momentum across countries, specifically in developing economies, to explore new business opportunities, innovation, entrepreneurial growth, and sustainable economic transformation through technology-based start-ups (Yin et al., 2019). The foundational elements for construction of digital infrastructure require broadband internet availability, data centers, AI hubs, and industrial networks to enable entrepreneurial operations by analyzing real-time data (Martín-Rojas et al., 2023). Digital infrastructure in entrepreneurial operations has improved the performance of information networks by increasing efficiency of resource allocation, optimizing information asymmetry, and reducing the cost, time, and risk (CTR) factors to enable entrepreneurial business models to adapt to dynamic business competitive ecosystem (Rajagopal, 2025). The entrepreneurship business dynamics (EBD) model explains managing

Rajagopal, A. Rajagopal, *Artificial Intelligence and Entrepreneurship*, Palgrave Studies of Entrepreneurship and Social Challenges in Developing Economies,
https://doi.org/10.1007/978-3-032-14904-6_5

competitive advantages in real time using digital platforms compatible to AI and ML to optimize its impact on micro-level entrepreneurial operations (Li et al., 2024a; Rajagopal, 2025).

Technology Infrastructure for Entrepreneurship

AI infrastructure planning for micro, small, and medium enterprises is a process of designing, managing, and optimizing both hardware and software components to support the AI and ML application platforms. This technical foundation provides required computational speed, power, storage, and networking resources for effective AI and workloads. Infrastructure planning for effective function of AI and ML platforms results in operational efficiency, scalability, and storage of data for decision making in an organizational system. A robust AI infrastructure plan for entrepreneurial functions relies on graphic processing units and tensor processing units to manage the AI workloads, speed, and data storage. In this process, high performance data storage devices are required to manage complex databases used in AI applications and ML platforms like enterprise resource planning (ERP) to enable quick data retrieval for analysis and decision making. The scalability of AI and ML applications requires advanced networking with high internet bandwidth connectivity and low-latency networking (LLN)[1] is a crucial requirement to manage the transfer of large volume of data between computing and storage nodes efficiently. The LLN enables minimizing the delay in data transfer between network and local devices and help in managing quick data transfers and reducing cyber-physical distance, optimizing in-flow of data traffic, and hardware efficiency, and enabling high speed connections streamlining the efficient path for data routine.

AI has significantly evolved as advanced machine- and deep learning models relying on symbolic methods programmed on machines to perform tasks on pre-defined rules. The major transformation of AI occurred with deep learning, which uses neural networks similar to human brain structure by recognizing natural language processing and predictive analysis. These features of AI applications provide advanced design thinking and computational power to disseminate contextual information to support entrepreneurial process (Floridi et al., 2018). Accordingly, AI in

[1] For details on LLN see www.hpe.com/us/en/what-is/low-latency.html retrieved on October 11, 2025.

entrepreneurship has significantly transformed entrepreneurial activities and decision making in developing technology-based business models. The AI-supported Big Data analysis enables entrepreneurs to integrate opportunities through generative and predictive analytics and develop dynamic capabilities to improve entrepreneurial performance in changing market ecosystems. AI also supports entrepreneurial decision-making process by reducing risk and increasing opportunities for corporate entrepreneurship to improve venture performance (Lee, 2020).

The emerging change in technology-enabled entrepreneurship has been found as platform-dependent entrepreneurship (PDE), which is growing gradually to support digital entrepreneurship. PDE provides venture score value creation by improving essential capabilities in managing technology, costs, and demand at real time (Cutolo & Kenney, 2021). Consequently, the PDE as a sub-category of digital entrepreneurship tends to reduce entrepreneurial uncertainty. The PDE is powered with generative AI providing support to entrepreneurs on real-time pricing, demand assessment, and value creation irrespective of swinging market traction. AI platforms with generative and predictive information support act as entrepreneurial catalyst and gatekeepers to optimize CTR factors within the blueprint of new venture creation (Hurni et al., 2022).

Innovation platform supported by AI enhances entrepreneurial design thinking and systematic manufacturing through modular architectures and provide effective governance structures to improve the performance of technology-based entrepreneurial ventures. PDE powered with generative AI effectively supports large language models (LLM) and user co-creations to provide real-time data through cloud infrastructure and opensource frameworks on public domain. Such transformation in technology accessibility has reduced the barriers for resource-constrained entrepreneurs enabling them to explore new pathways of capability oriented entrepreneurial activities (Giuggioli & Pellegrini, 2023). Accordingly, it can be stated that generative AI platforms have emerged as entrepreneurial catalysts and gatekeepers as they tend to expand entrepreneurial opportunities and enhance capability, streamline governance, and coevolve with changing industry and market ecosystems (Parker et al., 2017). The AI infrastructure along with PDE enables entrepreneurs to improve the combination of low-cost innovation and market attraction for utilitarian products to gain competitive advantage. Increasing efficiency and productivity using AI infrastructure can automate repetitive tasks, streamline processes, and improve transactional functions like logistics, marketing, and financial performance. The data-driven insights enable informed and proactive decisions from identifying opportunities to timely prediction of entrepreneurial risks. The AI- and PDE-based entrepreneurship can enhance customer experience by enabling customization of products and services by adding value to customer expectations. Technology-based entrepreneurship is convergent with NOISE comprising *need*-based assessment, exploring *opportunities*, continuous *innovation*, improving entrepreneurial *strengths*, and managing entrepreneurial outcomes to match customers, stakeholders, and business partners *expectation* (Rajagopal, 2026).

Technology administration balances business modeling and technology-based entrepreneurship through effective AI infrastructure planning for continuous information processing to support right decision making in enterprises as exhibited in Fig. 5.1. Technology administration in enterprises is central to management of information using AI and ML tools on various digital platforms to strategically manage business modeling and entrepreneurial operations to deliver business values responsibly to customers, stakeholders, and business partners. Effective technology administration relates to managing the information silos for making decisions on

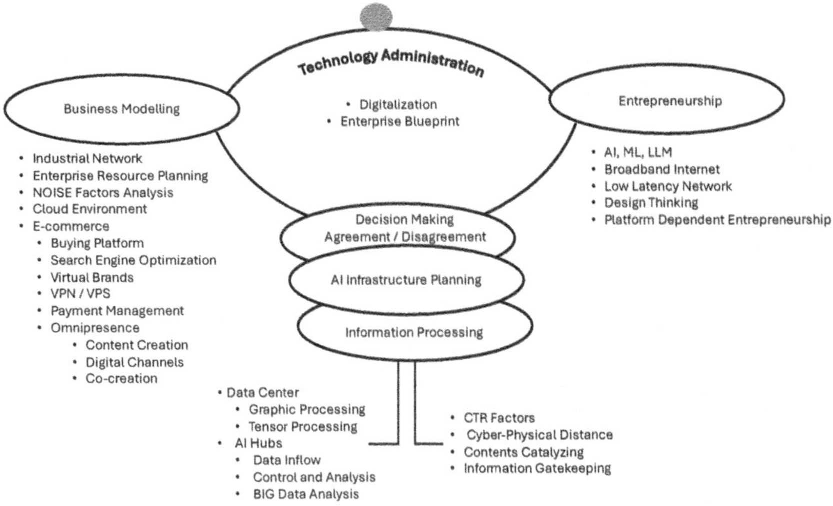

Fig. 5.1 Technology infrastructure for entrepreneurship and business modeling. (Source: Authors)

enterprise scalability, governance, and ethical integration of AI and ML across the technology applications and platforms. A robust AI administration framework enables digitization across entrepreneurial operations touchpoints through customized and efficient enterprise blueprint developed with clear vision, effective governance, and responsive team structure. The AI-based information support helps in reducing human oversight in entrepreneurial processes and reduces CTR factors by eliminating embedded risk and biases preventing firms from taking inappropriate business decisions.

Technology administration in developing efficiency in entrepreneurship requires integration of AI, ML, and LLM using broadband internet, which enables uninterrupted data flow from cloud environment through AI tools. Such synchronization improves the speed of information flow on low latency networks, which helps in managing platform dependent entrepreneurship for quick decision making on complex scenarios. In addition, technology administration through digitization, enterprise blueprint, and AI and ML tools improves the design thinking in micro, small, and medium enterprises to stay competitive in the marketplace. Integrating AI into risk management challenges lowers enterprise risk and compliances addressing the data breaches, misappropriation, alignment with regulatory measures, and eliminating data biases. However, the performance of AI and ML tools largely depends on data quality and data control administration through robust data governance system. This ensures clean, complete, and accessible databases for quick decision making. The seamless flow of data through AI and ML administration ensures data validation, data filtering, and data-based decision transformations. However, AI suggestions and outputs of ML platforms are often subjected to the agreements and disagreements of entrepreneurs based on authenticity and usability of data in making real-time decisions. Developing business models in PDEs require analytical application of AI for both qualitative and quantitative assessments of market ecosystem including analysis of consumer behavior. Language and sentiment AI enhances the behavioral dimensions in decision making by strengthening the automated inflow of information to eliminate data disputes, financial analysis, and behavioral compliances in refining business models to develop convergence with the market ecosystem (Nevi et al., 2025).

Integration of AI and ML into digital platforms manages data inflows and transfers within industrial networks to facilitate business modeling through cloud environment and create, deliver, and capture both qualitative and quantitative data with focus on industry and market related real-time scenarios as explained in Fig. 5.1. The enterprise resource planning platform for business modeling creates an integrated source of information analysis by aligning real-time scenarios with strategic business goals which improve efficiency, communication, and logical decision making. The ERP platforms are commonly supported by the software of Microsoft dynamic 360, oracle net suite, and similar tools. Strategic alignment of ERP platform enables mapping and synchronizing key activities of enterprises with strategic goals and ensure real-time decisions to gain competitive advantage. The clear workflows in ERP eliminate redundancies and insufficiencies of information with improved data integrity and consolidation of multi-variate information into a single unified system by eliminating the duplicity of information. These platforms enable shared view of data and processes to improve coordination across departments to facilitate appropriate decision making (Szopinski et al., 2020). Business modeling among micro, small, and medium enterprises have critical need for developing efficient e-commerce infrastructure by creating user friendly buying platforms and developing efficient visualization and ensure omnipresence by optimizing search engines to enable quick search with alternate product options to facilitate decision making. Using Al and ML platforms, these enterprises can also develop virtual brands with focus on sharing product attributes across digital channels and platforms. However, actions on cyber security need to be prioritized using virtual private networks (VPN) and virtual private servers (VPS) to protect vital stakeholder data (consumers and suppliers) and manage secured transactions through authentic payment gateways (Bresciani et al., 2021). The omnipresence of information across digital channels and platforms should be developed through core content creation and user generated content (co-created information).

Entrepreneurs often face critical challenges in efficiently managing information resources to develop product competitiveness by reducing CTR factors while maximizing the returns. Time, cost, and market information are the principle economic criteria for developing efficient business model. Therefore, information processing using data centers supported by AI and ML tools is critical to business modeling. The data centers can be broadly used for graphic processing and tensor processing through AI and ML tools. Tensor processing unit (TPU) is an application specific integrated circuit developed by google to accelerate the AI and ML workloads within neural network computations. TPUs excel in large scale applications used for speech recognition and real-time scenario translations to improve graphical maps within AI workloads. Information processing in entrepreneurial consortiums and guilds is conducted through AI hubs, which are centralized platforms for data locations that integrate various AI tools, frameworks, and resources to enable developing data-based business models with appropriate control and analysis. The principal AI hubs that support entrepreneurial consortiums are located in the United States (San Francisco, New York, and Boston) and Mexico (Tecnologico de Monterrey) for regional coverage of entrepreneurial consortiums.

The advantages of AI-based information processing include analyzing Big Data under various changing market scenarios to enable control of CTR factors and improving entrepreneurial profitability. The global information mapping and synchronizing data inflow across AI hubs and ML platforms help in reducing cyber-physical distance and manage real-time decision making for competitive advantage. Graphic and tensor information processing help in catalyzing core contents by geo-demographic segments and different market scenarios to align with consumer behavior and market requirements. Consequently, information gatekeeping at data centers and AI hubs facilitates real-time information processing to keep micro, small, and medium enterprises abreast with the market movements (Allweins et al., 2021).

Digital Marketing Infrastructure

Architecting an effective e-commerce firm complying with the requirements of technology infrastructure, besides identifying target audience, analyzing the existing market competition, setting up clear goals, choosing right suppliers, and appropriate marketing channels, is very essential. As e-commerce is all about user-efficient buying platforms, virtual store displays, order processing, and delivery management, it is important for the firms to optimize e-commerce website for search engines through the search engine optimization (SEO) process. SEO efficiency can be enhanced by adding relevant keywords, meta descriptions, and structured data to improve search efficacy and search engine ranking. An efficient business-to-consumers website must be able to create compelling product pages, streamline the checkout process, implement personalized marketing tactics, and track results to make necessary adjustments (Rajagopal, 2025).

Analyzing competitive strategies is another underlying challenge and firms must conduct research on the websites of the competing e-commerce firms, pricing, visual merchandising, and marketing strategies to develop differential marketing strategies to gain competitive advantage. Defining product-mix (product categories and product line), competitive features, quality, pricing, and positioning within the market enable firms to create a consistent brand image across all platforms, including logo, messaging, and tone of voice, which also helps in developing virtual brand identity. Nonetheless, a clean, intuitive website layout with easy navigation and quick loading time attracts the online buyers and enables them to navigate across the departments of the store to make appropriate buying decisions. Developing high-quality product pages including detailed product descriptions, high-resolution images, customer reviews, and clear size/color options encourages visual merchandising and improve the performance of e-commerce (Rajagopal, 2025).

Start-up e-commerce companies or a group of e-commerce companies may choose to share hosting of the web server with the principal server of the mother company. However, Virtual Private Server (VPS) provides better control over the data exchanges in business and resources as compared to the shared hosting for single client firms. Beyond the options discussed above, a dedicated server offers maximum control and resources, which is ideal for large e-commerce sites with heavy traffic. Another option for the web server is cloud hosting, which is both scalable and flexible, allowing firms to adjust resources based on demand and manage fluctuations in traffic and transactions. While setting up the web server for e-commerce, most firms face a major challenge to prioritize securities to safely manage sensitive customer data and protect the personal data from security breach and cyber-attacks. Data can be largely protected by implementing SSL certificates, firewalls, and regular security updates, using secured payment gateways, and complying with industry standards like Payment Card Industry Data Security Standard (PCI-DSS). PCI-DSS is a set of security standards designed to ensure that all e-commerce firms who accept, process, store, or transmit credit card information maintain a secure environment. This security measure helps in encrypting the transmission of cardholder data across open public networks. In addition to securing the electronic payment processes, firms also need to strengthen the inventory management system to track stock levels, manage orders, and optimize warehouse operations. Efficient inventory management is essential for meeting customer demand and minimizing costs. The shipping and fulfillment solutions manage the logistics of delivering products to customers. These solutions integrate with various carriers and provide real-time tracking to ensure timely and accurate deliveries (Rajagopal, 2025).

AI-Based Designing and Manufacturing

Design thinking and AI capabilities are transcending individual and conventional designing in dynamic markets today. The AI-based design thinking significantly influences the new product development designing and manufacturing process with agility in decision making and structured conditions facilitating development of trendy designs with effective implementation possibilities. Design thinking, as a dynamic capability driven by AI and ML tools, enables innovations by pooling design information, behavioral trends, market demand, and process agilities (Kyriakopoulos et al., 2025). Adoption of AI in business process and design thinking has transitioned the new product development process with competitive advantage and drive responsive solutions to consumer needs. Accordingly, the AI capabilities in enterprises help in boosting the new product development efforts and analyze trends to generate new ideas with AI-human interface that enable stakeholders and employees to engage in multidisciplinary tasks to develop appropriate designs by integrating information analytics and design coding expertise (Magistretti et al., 2021).

The AI-based design tools integrate the preconceived design maps with a view to increase efficiency, create intermittent ideas, and automate tasks with visual pallets and image editing support. AI-based designing increases efficiency in editing visuals and making layout adjustments to enhance product designing and creativity by generating design options based on contemporary trends and data. However, accurate designing in congruence with the real-time market trends using AI tools is complex due to changing consumer preferences and unstructured ethnic workflows that often disintegrate the automated suggestions while relying on manual interventions. AI-based graphic designing has effective workflows generating wide spectrum of color pallets and enhancing image quality to trigger new prototypes and brainstorming ideas to connect with AI tools and platforms. Notwithstanding the increasing relevance of AI tools and digital platforms, non-conventional design thinking, emerging technology-based enterprises encounter multi-faceted problems in conjunction with human-centeredness, conventional visualization, restructuring innovation activities, and withstanding the innovation experiments (Klenner et al., 2022).

AI reviews the evidence-based elements in design thinking and automating conventional process by considering user-centeredness and associated perceived values, which empower entrepreneurs to agree with AI suggestions for creating fast mover competitive advantages. Such cognitive synchronization with AI eliminates underlined biases in decision making and overcomes conventional inertia in design thinking conflicts. Accordingly, entrepreneurs tend to engage multiple stakeholders and users to map AI-based real-time designs for products and services to take a comparative look from different insights to integrate these designs into new product development process. Such alignment in design innovation projects with changing strategic goals strengthens the design thinking scenarios and aligns with visualization and prototyping of designs to gain competitive advantage (Meier & Kock, 2024).

The operational layout of AI-based design and process mapping enabling AI-decision making (DM) convergence broadly has two categorical dimensions comprising product design layers (PDL) and process design stages (PDS) as exhibited in Fig. 5.2. PDL has four layers including design thinking (L1), design efficiency (L2), design implementation (L3), and commercialization (L4) that emerges as an outcome of carrying out AI intervention through the six stages of PDS, which includes managing

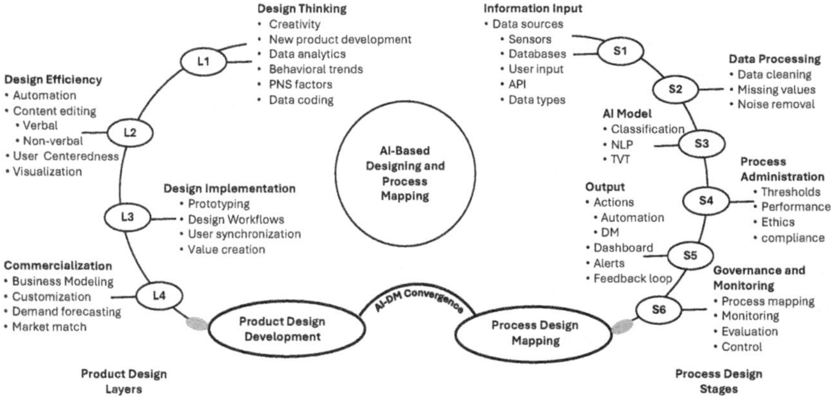

Fig. 5.2 Layout of AI-based designing and process mapping. (Source: Authors)

information output (S1), data processing (S2), AI modeling (S3), process administration (S4), output (S5), and governance and monitoring (S6).

Design thinking (L1) is largely driven by co-intelligence, a combination of entrepreneurial experience, cognition, and knowledge, along with the AI-based creativity in developing competitive designs for new product development. The AI intervention in entrepreneurial product designing process requires information pooling in the context of real-time data and market trends, behavioral trends of users, and analysis of PNS factors to enable creative layouts of product designs through data analytics and data coding for ML platforms. The design thinking layer leads to the design efficiency layer (L2) in which AI and ML tools can be used for automation, and content editing (verbal and non-verbal) to build high impact visualization contextual to user-centeredness of new product development. Proceeding further on product design layers, design implementation (L3) opens a major challenge of developing design prototype and mapping design workflows to synchronize with user applications to create value as illustrated in Fig. 5.2. Commercialization (L4) of product design as a final layer of PDL stances is a major challenge among entrepreneurs in developing dynamic business models by analyzing real-time demand forecast and managing customization of new product designs to ensure an appropriate market match.

Convergence of product-design development and process-design mapping is managed through AI for decision making as a visual and collaborative method that enables teams to define the product design and process mapping requirements to optimize the new product development through ideation to commercialization stages. The process design on AI and ML platforms broadly comprises stages that include information, data processing, AI model selection, governance and monitoring, output management, and model implementation. The information input (S1) requires pooling information from various data sources through sensors, cloud-based data bases, and user inputs across different data types subjected to application programming interface (API), which is instrumental in determining key metrics to measure effectiveness of processes. The quality of data input enhances operational efficiencies by optimizing process development time, reducing time of repetitive cycles, and enhancing circular feedback of customers. Data processing (S2) helps process design teams understand the process requirement, flow of tasks, and critical decision points in classifying, cleaning, providing missing values, and noise removal from raw data. Data processing is an essential stage to select AI model (S3) by appropriate classification, natural language processing (NLP), and integrating TVT elements comprising training, validation, and testing of data through selected AI models. The digital tools like Miro can facilitate firms in collaborative mapping. Selection of appropriate AI models can increase efficiency by visualizing the process maps, managing CTR factors, reducing transitional waste, and streamlining the workflow. The AI-powered assistants like Virtual assistant or Copilot significantly contribute to lean process improvement during the product design and process mapping phases to develop balanced workloads and eliminate redundancies in tasks.

Governance and monitoring (S4) can be categorically managed in process mapping by categorizing the thresholds of processes to measure performance and compliances following ethical codes. For example, BMW, a German automaker optimizes industrial planning and supply chain using both generative and predictive AI in a synchronous environment to refine production workflows and regulate production cycles for new products (vehicles). The product design output (S5) structure streamlines actions, automation, and decision making by visualizing process design mapping on dashboards integrating process alerts and feedback loops between the stages. Audi, a German automaker, critically analyzes the outputs to streamline the global sourcing processes and value chain management to implement AI-based models (S6) efficiently the process maps by exercising stage-gate-based monitoring, evaluation, and control.

The conceptual overview of AI-based products and process design maps typically includes various stages that can be identified as input layers, data processing, AI model layer, decision layer, and output layer. AI tools identify appropriate data sources, analyze databases and user input, and synchronize application program interface (API) which serves as a crucial mechanism for accessing and integrating data from various sources. Establishing input layer and data structuring, managing unstructured text images, and semi-structured data are analyzed in the AI-based designing process. In addition, data enhancement sensors including verbal and non-verbal elements are also integrated at this stage. The silos of cloud-based data require continuous cleaning by removing biases, redundancies, and providing missing values. These tasks are managed in the second stage of AI-based product and process designing maps. AI works with featured data engineering inputs by integrating data labeling for monitoring verbal and non-verbal contents and extracting meaningful features. This second stage leads to the AI model layer in the third stage by engaging classification of data, computation, clustering, natural language processing, and integrating computer vision into chronological data. Such sequencing helps in design model selection and measuring the accuracy, precision, and recall of data-based verbal and non-verbal designs for validation and testing. In the fourth stage of AI-based product and process mapping, the real time or batch predictions are performed within the logical thresholds of business requirements. The decision layer in AI designing process allows human-in-the-loop actions for optional reviews and overriding conventional bottlenecks before agreeing to AI product and design suggestions. The fifth stage is based on mapping automated decisions, alerts, contextual suggestions, dashboard formations, refining visualizations, and analyzing feedback loop for continuous learning in conceptualization and implementation of AI-based product designs and process maps. The governance and monitoring of AI-based products and process maps require drift detection as a practice to monitor models and designs in production to identify and alert their performance shrinkage. It's also necessary at this stage to eliminate biases in design and reinforce data privacy and excess control.

Broadly, AI-based designing can be explained as mimicking human cognitive processes by analyzing perception, logic, problem-solving abilities, and creativity to match with the real-time data and automation process. As AI demonstrates automated design thinking based on natural language processing, the suggested product and process maps are synchronized with human-in-the-loop process to reinforce interaction and creativity. Conventionally, creativity and repetitive design process are human-centered approaches, which have been revolutionized by AI providing intelligent solutions and automation of activities based on synchronous (real-time) data (Mahato et al., 2021). The potential of generative AI enables new design creation with verbal and non-verbal data augmenting human creativity and overcoming conventional challenges. In the early decades of twenty-first century, most creative entrepreneurial firms such as IKEA and LEGO used crowdsourcing and idea competitions involving crowd-based inputs to refine innovative designs at real time. However, human centricity in real-time designing has faced challenges converging them with production efficiencies by reducing CTR factors and increasing market competitiveness. The generative AI has promoted divergent thinking by challenging human biases, assisting in new idea evaluation, synchronizing ideas with production process, and aligning with the real-time market trends (Eapen et al., 2023).

Collective Intelligence and Digital Networks

Crowd creativity provides rich and applied manifestation of ideas, working strategies (draft), and user-generated contents to solve problems. However, such solutions largely remain untested and stand on hypothetical grounds, which poses risks in developing and implementing prima facie public strategies due to social and legal risks associated with the 3I-elements comprising impulsive ideation, situation interpretations and infringement of intellectual property. Consequently, companies relying on crowd-based business modeling need to explore possibility of digital rights management to stand clear on the intellectual property issues while prospecting the crowdsourcing of solutions. Crowd-based information needs to be validated against the risks of using intellectual property and strategic-fit on the business performance perspectives. Crowds commonly deliver raw information, which mitigates the risks associated with soliciting solutions to any uncommon or less occurring problem associated with the products and services. The unrefined crowd information is commonly proactive, premature, possessive, and persuasive, which needs to be judged within the social and business ecosystems (de Beer et al., 2017; Rajagopal, 2021).

Advancement of information technology has been radically adapted to social and frugal innovations. The crowdfunding process has been leveraged by such technology advancement. Over time, companies evaluate the threats and opportunities of crowdfunding and create new business options for the more-connected future of digital ecosystems. Consequently, many social innovation companies such as Uber, Airbnb, and Amazon are doing business successfully with the support of digitization, which offered opportunities for companies to leverage strong customer relationships and increase cross-selling. Simultaneously, many companies are deriving real value from social business using social media, social software, and technology-based social networks to enable relationships among people, information, and social capital. Social businesses play important role in decision making to maintain the quality of life in most rural and sub-urban population segments. It is estimated in some research studies that incremental improvements to the existing social business practices contribute to positive business outcomes, and deliver benefits associated with the social business at the stage of maturity. The continuous improvement in social businesses requires a substantial change (Kane et al., 2014; Rajagopal, 2021).

AI and Supply Chain Management

The cloud-based technology interactions in various supply chain management (SCM) process among micro, small, and medium enterprises has been significantly transformed with the usage of AI-based information tools, digital platforms, and supply chain networks. The intervention of AI has leveraged the efficiency of SCM processes by analyzing large data sets enabling entrepreneurs to make faster and resilient decisions. Transiting from manual logistics and inventory process to automated environment, the risk of transitional bottlenecks and dynamic inventory management has been significantly reduced using AI tools. The technology-SCM interface in AI environment ensures end-to-end visibility, optimization of process efficiency, reducing CTR factors, and enables augmenting entrepreneurial decisions to gain competitive advantage. The use of AI applications and adoption of technology-driven platforms streamlines SCM collaborations from procurement to delivery status and strengthens the trust in the SCM process with required robustness to improve sustainable performance (Liu et al., 2025).

The AI applications SCM process principally help in improving planning and forecasting, real-time logistics and transportation, and operational efficiency, with reduced risk factors. AI analyzes large historical data, market trends, and real-time information derived from digital networks, operational domains of transportation and logistics, and weather forecast to predict demand for supplies and real-time deliveries. Use of AI tools in SCM optimizes the work breakdown structure by streamlining production and supply schedules and resource allocations based on forecasted demand, production capacity, order processing, and delivery priorities to stay competitive in managing supplies at the client's doorsteps. Automated monitoring of inventory levels, order pattern, and analyzing profiles of both third-party suppliers and clients, AI enables streamlining the SCM process. The supply chain resilience has two embedded factors comprising supply chain resistance and supply chain recovery, which are crucial to the SCM process and can be managed efficiently with the transition of manual process to AI-based applications. The supply chain resistance refers to sustaining external shocks such as demand fluctuations or logistics disruptions, while the supply chain recovery is contextual to the performance of SCM to restore functional normality by adjusting business model and optimizing resource allocations (Tukamuhabwa et al., 2015).

One of the major challenges in logistics and transportation operations across different sizes of enterprises and business scales is the optimization of supply chain route, last line delivery, and warehouse monitoring. Entrepreneurs can ensure real-time route optimization by analyzing the traffic, weather, and fluctuations in delivery factors by using AI applications and analyzing real-time data. In addition, AI enables last line delivery scheduling by reducing the complexity of routes and delivery locations, and aligning with hub-and-spoke model, which contributes to streamlining first-in-first-out operations, managing vehicle capacities, and synchronizing deliveries to real-time orders. The decentralization of warehouse and inventory management by creating intermittent hubs has emerged as one of the simplified solutions to manage IDT system comprising inventory, delivery, and transportation system within critical SCM paths. AI-powered robotics enables inventory categorization, identifying critical supply paths, and determining CTR factors.

Walmart has developed a distribution system in which goods are first sent to large regional distribution centers (RDCs) and then dispatched to individual stores, which is known as a hub-and-spoke network model. Walmart efficiently moves goods from suppliers to the end-users, both in-store and online, using cross-docking as a part of the hub-and-spoke network. The hub and spoke distribution network are a centralized warehousing and shipping strategy where goods are initially docked at a central hub (a warehouse or distribution center) and then distributed outwards to various spoke locations (network warehouses, retail stores, or customer addresses). From these locations, goods are either delivered directly to customers or shipped to their destination through the layered stores of Walmart. This method resembles the spokes of a bicycle wheel radiating from the hub. By consolidating shipments and using predetermined distribution routes, Walmart streamlined the entire supply chain with the hub and spoke network. The business trajectory of Walmart experienced tremendous growth and changes from 1962 when the first store opened (e.g., Wang, 2023).

The inbound logistics are managed by the centralized warehouses of Walmart. Suppliers ship goods to RDCs, which are strategically located across the operational regions to minimize transportation costs and time and streamline the flow of goods. The company also has Import Distribution Centers (IDCs) that serve as receiving points for goods from designated ports and often hold inventory until demanded at the RDCs. The RDCs form the core of the distribution network to ensure efficient and rapid delivery to its local stores. Upon processing the inventory at the RDCs, they are forwarded to Walmart stores and for catering to the online orders. The company employs a fleet of trucks to deliver supplies to stores and manage online order fulfillment including localized home deliveries and click and pick orders. Walmart is taking several initiatives to continue its hold on grocery retailing despite increasing competition in the brick-and-mortar, online, and hybrid stores. Walmart has been aggressively pursuing click-and-collect models where customers buy an item online and pick it up at the store (Jindal et al., 2021; Rajagopal, 2025).

Technology has significantly contributed to modern distribution management by enhancing operational efficiency, process transparency, and suppliers' responsiveness encouraging the firms to use technology-driven tools comprising Artificial Intelligence (AI), Internet of Things (IoT), blockchain technology supported by radio frequency identification (RFID), and cloud computing. These technological tools enable firms in real-time tracking, conduct predictive analytics, optimized routing, and streamlining warehouse operations, improving customer satisfaction, and supply chain resilience. AI and ML algorithms are used for demand forecasting, route optimization, and automating tasks to prioritize order processing and delivery. Consequently, firms can develop accuracy in inventory management, reduce transportation costs, and faster delivery by reducing the cost-time-risk (CTR) factors (Rajagopal, 2025).

Digital technologies enable firms to track real-time movements in inventory and logistics operations and real-time surveillance through monitoring of inventory, shipments, and deliveries across the distribution network. The dynamic visibility allows firms to improve efficiency over the conventional approaches by proactively identifying issues, managing exceptions, and making data-driven decisions to optimize the distribution process. IoT devices also enable real-time tracking of goods and vehicles, providing visibility throughout the supply chain. This allows firms to make proactive adjustments to inventory levels and delivery schedules minimizing delays and disruptions. IoT devices like sensors and RFID tags support collection of data on selected indicators about products, equipment, and assets engaged in the distribution network and processes. Collected data can be utilized to optimize inventory levels, monitor conditions such as temperature and humidity in the silos or warehouses, and manage the floor layout and space related issues. In addition, IoT also helps firms in predictive maintenance of equipment and control the inventory damages (Rajagopal, 2025).

The predictive capability of AI significantly enhances the ability of enterprises to manage demand fluctuations and disruptions related to SCM by analyzing data from IoT network, cloud computing, and digital network-based market trends to foster SCM flexibility at local and global supply chains in a systematic manner. Predictive maintenance by using sensor data on AI and ML platforms allows entrepreneurs to schedule proactive tracking within the CTR limits. The computer vision systems powered by AI enable quality control in SCM process in real-time on diverse assembly lines and ensure operations with lower costs spill, operational waste, and reworking on tasks. Such intervention of AI helps in identifying potential disruptions in advance by advising decision makers to develop contingency plans and enhance SCM resilience (Papadopoulos et al., 2017).

RFID technology in supply chain management enhances automation and provides real-time tracking of goods to improve inventory management. It enables accuracy in data collection to develop plans for optimized routing with minimal errors. RFID tags attached to products or containers allow for continuous tracking of goods throughout the supply chain, from procurement to manufacturing and retail. RFID systems provide precise inventory counts, reducing errors and improving accuracy. A combination of RFID and blockchain technology is a powerful strategy that can be used to enhance supply chain management, asset tracking, and overall business efficiency in logistics. RFID tags, which serve as digital identification cards for goods enable real-time tracking and provide location updates. Blockchain then provides a secure, transparent, and permanent record of these transactions and information, creating a trustworthy and auditable data system. This synergy of technological tools leads to improved traceability, cost reduction, and streamlined logistics, inventory, and supply chain operations. Consequently, use of RFID helps firms in automating various supply chain tasks comprising ordering, processing, storage, logistics, and distribution by minimizing the labor cost, human errors, and improving efficiency (Rajagopal, 2025).

Semantic Methods for Business Processes

Technology-based firms tend to use ontologies and semantic web services to interpret ML-led business process central to the semantic methods for business process management (SBPM). Semantic methods bridge high order business goals and underline challenges of technology implementation to drive automation and agility in business process life cycle. SBMP is often created in machine language like business process modeling notation (BPMN), which enables business models to be machine understandable and compatible with automated reasoning (Remco et al., 2008). Ontologies in business are commonly defined as standardized terminology such as invoices, order processing, customers, and deliveries. The data pertaining to ontologies is processed in natural language text descriptions with semantic annotations allowing the reuse of data on ML platforms, which significantly reduces the human repetitive tasks (Di Martino et al., 2023). SBPM helps also in auto completion of data gaps by understanding the coding environments and auto-completion of terms for further automated analysis to support new decision loops. The advancement of technology could explore the semantic web services (SWS) by annotating the process tasks within common ontological concepts (Bertoli et al., 2022).

The SWS repository helps in bridging automatic composition gaps, which ontological concepts to override manual errors and conduct automated data mediation to resolve the inter-operability issues. In addition, semantic reasoning provides automated logical inference to exhibit implicit knowledge from explicit facts stored in the ontology-based repository. Visualization of semantics connects data using global key indicators from diverse sources explored and collected by AI tags for appropriate data analytics to support decision making and complex business scenarios. Process mining and discovery helps in integrating semantic techniques to analyze event logs (cause and effect, probable scenarios, business dynamics, and agile ecosystem). Semantic methods therefore enable seamless communication between heterogeneous systems by aligning process semantics across AI and ML platforms. The SBPM is effectively applied in supply chain management, healthcare workflows, financial systems, e-commerce, and e-governance systems. Broadly, SBPM focuses on increasing the degree of automation in developing, implementation, and monitoring of business processes with the AI and ML tools that support the SWS. The semantic process helps in organizing knowledge to develop process models through visualization, alignment of natural language, mapping and translation of data, identifying exceptional workflows, and process automation (Hoang et al., 2010).

The phenomenon of 'seeing is experiencing' is founded on the maxims of visual perceptions, which leads to cognitive reasoning and developing perceptions on visual objects. The visual data is analyzed within internal neural space, forms perceptual images, and drives cognitive reasoning through perceptual motions. The theories of visual perceptions argue that visual objects are perceived through neural networks and cognitive brain imaging to develop contextual semantics and decision making by the subjects. Visual perceptions are often sensitive to judgements, as inadequate construction of visual scenarios generates a gap between cognitive actualization and deception. Visual perceptions are affected by the quality of construction of visual scenario, cognitive inhibition, speed of visuals, and the combination of verbal (dynamic text) and non-verbal (contextual image, color, music, graphics, and appearance of anchors) elements. The scientific development on theory of visual perceptions has indicated several neural space dynamisms in mapping visual perceptions through visual pathways, optic tract, and topographical images (Jerath et al., 2018) within visual space. Visual perceptions are stimulated by motion and dynamics, and oscillatory activities. These factors drive the brain activity for visual processing, decomposing information, and analyzing the effects of visual consciousness (Rajagopal, 2025).

The theories of visual perceptions argue that visual objects are perceived through neural networks and cognitive brain imaging to develop contextual semantics and decision making by the subjects. Visual perceptions are often sensitive to judgements, as inadequate construction of visual scenarios generates a gap between cognitive actualization and deception. Visual perceptions are affected by the quality of construction of visual scenario, cognitive inhibition, speed of visuals, and the combination of verbal (dynamic text) and non-verbal (contextual image, color, music, graphics, and appearance of anchors) elements. The scientific development on theory of visual perceptions has indicated several neural space dynamisms in mapping visual perceptions through visual pathways, optic tract, and topographical images (Jerath et al., 2018) within visual space. Visual perceptions are stimulated by motion and dynamics, and oscillatory activities (Rajagopal & Rajagopal, 2023).

Emotional Modeling

Emotional modeling in business is a blend of understanding customer cognition and real-time decision making by blending with systematic representation and analysis of customer cognition, crowd behavior, and collective intelligence. Emotional modeling significantly improves the organizational outcomes by integrating AI and ML tools in real-time data analytics of consumer behavior to gain deeper insights into PNS factors portraying consumer behavior, employee engagement, and market dynamics. As AI technologies are transcending into business-to-business, business-to consumer, and hybrid business segments, the emotional modeling in business has turned complex behaviors into streamlined understanding leveraging design thinking, innovation, and services delivery. The emotional richness of consumers in the context of individual and group behavior, crowd perspectives, and holistic social appeals have emerged as promising tools for transforming the business landscape modeling by developing congruence with customization, streamlined operations, AI-based understanding, and digital support expansion (Gonçalves et al., 2024).

Emotional modeling is built on behavioral frameworks and AI-generated algorithms that simulate probable human emotions based on chronological behavioral data of consumers, biometric inputs, and crowd behavior. AI-based data also critically analyzes social conventions, PNS factors, **k**nowledge, **a**daptability, and **p**ractice experiences (KAP), and CARO comprising **c**onsistency, **a**ccuracy, **r**eliability, and **o**utput. The common approaches in interpreting human emotions through AI tools include affective computing, which detects non-verbal emotions by analyzing facial expressions, voice tone, and neurobehavioral signals. The affective computing enables carrying out sentiment analysis to measure individual or group human sentiments by analyzing the text data from IoT sources (data text mining). Synchronizing affective computing and content analysis leads to behavioral modeling inferring the individual and crowd emotional states to map behavioral patterns and support decision making in business.

AI significantly contributes to emotional modeling, which involves creating data-based algorithms to simulate and interpret human emotions by analyzing behavioral data, biometric inputs, anthropomorphic concepts, and social behavior. The common approach is to develop emotional modeling is found in carrying out affective computing by using sensors to detect neurobehavioral emotions from various human-body sensitive touch points, voice tone, and physiological signals. Emotional modeling is carried out in neuromonitoring experiments by analyzing the brain signals that impact physiological changes in consumer behavior. Such neurophysical and behavioral changes determine the consumer purchase intentions for a given product in a predetermined situation. The behavioral analysis is integrated with sentiment analysis by treating text data collected from social media and crowd repositories to measure the crowd cognition, chaos, and public sentiments. There are many technological platforms to manage emotional modeling with AI and ML tools and interpret results across multiple business functions (Li et al., 2024b).

Among some platforms, IBM Watson tone analyzer conducts data text mining and analyzes return text to detect emotional tones such as happiness, anger, sadness, and confidence to derive appropriate behavioral conclusions that are useful for managing customer services, marketing, and market communications. The text analytics can also be conducted on Microsoft Azure platform, which offers sentiment scoring for text inputs and help decision makers to understand customer feedback and crowd sentiments. Cogito is another platform, which provides real-time emotional intelligence by analyzing voice tone and client conversation patterns to guide agents to improve customer interactions, establish authenticity, and provide necessary solutions. This AI-driven software is commonly used by business call centers to provide virtual customer assistance. MetLife, a US-based insurance company, deployed AI tools of Cogito in call centers to provide real-time coaching to the agents and analyzing customer emotions using AI, which guided call center agents to respond empathetically to customer issues resulting in an increase in resolving issues, customer satisfaction, and reduction in call handling time. This strategy exhibited the benefits of emotional modeling in improving service quality and operational efficiency.[2]

The omnipresence strategy of products and services across digital channels and platforms strengthens emotional relationships across neurobehavioral touchpoints of consumers by determining critical strategic priorities. Connecting with AI assistants, firms can improve behavioral proximity to consumers and enrich digital interactions by providing personalized suggestions, real-time scenario support, and AI-human interface to nurture interactive cognition. The AI-based emotional business modeling has become central to customer-centric strategies with distinctiveness and delivering socially meaningful experiences. Consequently, the AI-based emotional modeling in business significantly drives deeper knowledge, affective benefits, and immersive experience through technology tools like AR, VR, and MR (Sestino et al., 2022). Customer facing strategies can be developed to build an emotional business model and gain competitive

[2]For details on the benefits of emotional modeling see https://www.marketingscoop.com/ai/emotional-ai-examples/ (retrieved on October 20, 2025).

advantage by customer-centric firms. In this process, emotional branding and empathy-driven design constitute major contributions as they outgrow customer's feelings, needs, and expectations to drive buying decisions. Such emotional branding generates emotional attachment and cognitive bonding with the attributes of brand, etymology, social value and lifestyle, and brand promise. Embedding consumer emotions into design thinking process to cater to empathy-driven brand designing through AI tools helps firms to identify contextual touchpoints of brand and consumers to deliver valuable and meaningful solutions.

Emotional business modeling dives deep into psychological, neurobehavioral, and cognitive ecosystems by stimulating memories, nostalgia, and episodic experiences that drive loyalty and repeat purchase behavior with significant emotional signals. AI-based behavioral analytics provides impactful decision-making opportunities through emotional connect and analyzing crowd cognitive metrics to stimulate customer association, loyalty, and retention. The emotional business modeling exhibits competitive differentiation with AI-human interface providing enhanced scope of business, innovation, and profit-with-purpose (Kim et al., 2020). The contribution of generating AI in analyzing and disseminating real-time verbal and non-verbal data including text and images has significantly influenced the cognitive process, emotional responses, real-time learning, contextual sensitivity, and motivational engagement in understanding consumers, stakeholders, and business partners to develop business models with emotional inputs (Lin et al., 2024).

The ability to influence consumer emotions related to brands through virtual reality has affected individual attitudes and generated awareness about changing the collective behavior toward e-commerce and virtual business platforms (Fauville et al., 2020; Rajagopal, 2025). Virtual business integrating virtual shopping today is a latitudinal approach, which enhances the outreach of customers through effective consumer advocacy, diffusion of collective intelligence, and influencing consumers through the crowd behavior. Due to the increasing dependency on social media marketing and network marketing trend, the latitudinal proximity in business markets is rapidly reducing. Such shifts in consumer marketing have significantly affected the buying behavior of consumers (Tiwary et al., 2021; Rajagopal, 2025). The ChatGPT has the new AI revolution in the public domain to develop interactive relationships and mutual dependency to learn and widen the information silos. AI robots serve as co-workers and analysts for decision making in large multi-brand and international customer-centric firms. AI has yet to support tourism and hospitality industry robots with trust, anticipation, and emotions. Happiness, arousal, and merriment have a significant impact on robot sentiment polarity, while anticipation and surprise do not significantly affect the AI logarithms. Therefore, one major challenge is to anthropomorphize robots for tourism and hospitality industry (Jörling et al., 2019; Rajagopal, 2025).

Emotions in business modeling attract psychodynamics, a cognitive process of consumers, which is induced by digital or personal word-of-mouth and shared use value on products or services among consumers. The psychodynamics on the perceived use value of the products or services affect both the conscious and unconscious states if mind, which develops push and pull effects in the business. It also plays significantly with the consumer emotions and crowd behavior for a brand. Positive psychodynamics among consumers creates pull-effect for specific brands in the market. The pull-effect generates high consumer demand which benefits companies in increasing market share and profit by reducing the marketing costs. Such costs for brands are spread across advertisements, in-store promotions, price discounts, and point-of-sales incentives to the consumers (Rajagopal, 2019). Visualization stimulates human emotions and business strategies with AI-driven visualization enabling neuro-behavioral stimulation, emotions, and purchase intentions among consumers. To customize visualization of products on e-commerce platforms firms must collect data of consumer choices about the verbal and non-verbal contents, use values, price, process, promotion, customer reviews, colors, images, videos, and the like. Firms can prepare databases and update them periodically to create website graphics and charts using static or animation tools. Data visualization for e-commerce is fundamentally a graphical representation of product and consumer information. By using visual elements like charts, graphs, and maps, data visualization tools provide an accessible way to see and understand trends, outliers, and patterns in data. Data visualization helps in exhibiting complex information in an organized way (Rajagopal, 2021).

Case Study

CS1: HubSpot and Motion AI

HubSpot is a technology company integrated with AI and ML services, which provides software applications to support marketing and sales functions besides the customized CRM platform for small and medium size businesses. The company has created in-bound technology for marketing and successfully used Web2.0 technology to provide CRM services and strategies to enhance the existing customer base of affiliated firms including small and medium businesses. HubSpot has rose into prominence during the COVID-19 pandemic period as most firms had aggressively adapted to the digital platforms of HubSpot and integrated AI services to compete in the digital business ecosystem (Joshi & Burgelman, 2025).

Overtime, technologies with AI have significantly grown upon acquisition of motion AI company by HubSpot in 2017. Software-as-a-service (SaaS) companies like HubSpot have driven generative AI as a major development, which impacted marketing and sales processes in hyper personalization and contextual content generation to provide AI-driven chatbots to enable managers to improve business development perspectives and competitive sales prospects through AI-driven sales funnels. The chatbots configured as information agents of sales funnel have focused on developing competitive sales strategies and creating customer value to gain market leadership and competitive advantage. However, among other challenges, the company faced AI-customer relationship dilemmas with focus on agreements and disagreements to AI-generated contents and chatbot conversations with customers, stakeholders, employees, and business partners (Avery, 2024). HubSpot aimed at developing strategic objectives to cater automated customer interactions across its CRM platforms to reduce response time and improve lead qualifications. However, the company encountered a major challenge of ensuring chatbots to display and simulate human-like empathy and responsiveness.

HubSpot integrated motion AI into its digital prospects and opportunities with Growth Stack encompassing many platforms including as follows:

- HubSpot CRM (real-time data analytics and visual dashboard)
- Marketing hub (media content analysis, e-mail marketing, and communication automation)
- Sales hub (customer outreach, activity scheduling, and sales analytics)
- Services hub (customer retention and loyalty)
- Content hub (AI-driven content management and search engine optimization tools)

- Operations hub (data synchronization, filtering, and streamlining operations)

HubSpot has deployed chatbots across websites, Facebook managers, slack, and SMS engines as a part of Growth Stack. The chatbots are programmed to demonstrate quality leads, provide customer support, and suggest personalized sales funnels to support emotional modeling through anthropomorphic bots, which exhibited human like traits. These chatbots have significantly influenced customer's trust and generated satisfaction by carrying out AI-driven analytics to experience emotional depth in customer relationship management. The joint efforts of HubSpot and motion AI could increase the marketing leads in competitive business by reducing the CTR factors while the chatbots programmed by the company reduced the wait time and provided real time and continuous support to enhance customer experience by scaling-up the emotional engagement. Open-ended interactions have enabled comprehensive understanding of customers through descriptive responses at various levels of emotional intelligence in different real-time scenarios. However, customer expectations did not acknowledge the anthropomorphic visions of the chatbots as they lacked human-like emotions and largely demonstrated scripted responses to open ended interactions. Such limitation has raised questions on emotional design of chatbots by aligning AI to develop empathetic human behavior and foster behavioral strength and trust. In addition, combining chatbots with human agents across the sales funnel had major challenges to ensure both efficiency and emotional depth.

References

Allweins, M. M., Proesch, M., & Ladd, T. (2021). The platform canvas-conceptualization of a design framework for multi-sided platform businesses. *Entrepreneurship Education and Pedagogy, 4*, 455–477.

Avery, J. (2024). *HubSpot and motion AI (B): Generative AI opportunities.* Harvard Business School Press. 524-088.

Bertoli, P., Corcoglioniti, F., Francescomarino, C. D., Dragoni, M., Ghidini, C., & Pistore, M. (2022). Semantic modeling and analysis of complex data-aware processes and their executions. *Expert Systems with Applications, 198*. https://doi.org/10.1016/j.eswa.2022.116702

Bresciani, S., Huarng, K.-H., Malhotra, A., & Ferraris, A. (2021). Digital transformation as a springboard for product, process and business model innovation. *Journal of Business Research, 128*, 204–210.

Cutolo, D., & Kenney, M. (2021). Platform-dependent entrepreneurs: Power asymmetries, risks, and strategies in the platform economy. *Academy of Management Perspectives, 35*(4), 584–605.

de Beer, J., McCarthy, I. P., Soliman, A., & Treen, E. (2017). Click here to agree: Managing intellectual property when crowdsourcing solutions. *Business Horizons, 60*(2), 207–217.

Di Martino, B., Cante, C. L., Esposito, A., & Graziano, M. (2023). A tool for the semantic annotation, validation and optimization of business process models. *Software: Practice and Experience., 53*(5), 1174–1195.

Eapen, T. T., Finkenstadt, D. J., Folk, J., & Venkataswamy, L. (2023). How generative AI can augment human creativity. *Harvard Business Review, 101*(4), 56–64. https://hbr.org/2023/07/how-generative-ai-can-augment-human-creativity

Fauville, G., Muller Queiroz, A. C., & Bailenson, J. N. (2020). In J. Kim & H. Song (Eds.), *Virtual reality as a promising tool to promote climate change awareness* (pp. 91–108). Technology and Health, Academic Press.

Floridi, L., Cowls, J., Beltrametti, M., Chatila, R., Chazerand, P., Dignum, V., Luetge, C., Madelin, R., Pagallo, U., & Rossi, F. (2018). AI4People—An ethical framework for a good AI society: Opportunities, risks, principles, and recommendations. *Minds Machines, 28*, 689–707.

Giuggioli, G., & Pellegrini, M. M. (2023). Artificial intelligence as an enabler for entrepreneurs: A systematic literature review and an agenda for future research. *International Journal of Entrepreneurial Behavior & Research, 29*(4), 816–837.

Gonçalves, A. R., Costa Pinto, D., Shuqair, S., Mattila, A., & Imanbay, A. (2024). The paradox of immersive artificial intelligence (AI) in luxury hospitality: How immersive AI shapes consumer differentiation and luxury value. *International Journal of Contemporary Hospitality Management, 36*(11), 3865–3888.

Hoang, H. H., Tran, P. C. T., & Le, T. M. (2010). *State of the art of semantic business process management: An investigation on approaches for business-to-business integration.* In N. T. Nguyen, M. T. Le, & J. Świątek (Eds.), *Intelligent Information and Database Systems. ACIIDS 2010. Lecture notes in computer science, 5991.* Springer.

Hurni, T., Huber, T. L., & Dibbern, J. (2022). Power dynamics in software platform ecosystems. *Information Systems Journal, 32*(2), 310–343.

Jerath, R., Cearley, S. M., Barnes, V. A., & Jensen, M. (2018). Micro-calibration of space and motion by photoreceptors synchronized in parallel with cortical oscillations: A unified theory of visual perception. *Medical Hypotheses, 110*, 71–75.

Jindal, R. P., Gauri, D. K., Li, W., & Ma, Y. (2021). Omnichannel battle between Amazon and Walmart: Is the focus on delivery the best strategy? *Journal of Business Research, 122*, 270–280.

Jörling, M., Böhm, R., & Paluch, S. (2019). Service robots: Drivers of perceived responsibility for service outcomes. *Journal of Service Research, 22*(4), 404–420. https://doi.org/10.1177/1094670519842334

Joshi, R., & Burgelman, R. (2025). *HubSpot in 2025: Inspiring SMBs from the internet age to the AI era*. Harvard Business School Press.

Kane, G. C., Palmer, D., Phillips, A. N., & Kiron, D. (2014). Finding the value in social business. *MIT Sloan Management Review, 55*(3), 81–88.

Kim, J., Merrill, K., Jr., & Collins, C. (2020). Touchdown together: Social TV viewing and social presence in a physical co-viewing context. *The Social Science Journal, 61*(*3*), 1–15.

Klenner, N. F., Gemser, G., & Karpen, I. O. (2022). Entrepreneurial ways of designing and designerly ways of entrepreneuring: Exploring the relationship between design thinking and effectuation theory. *Journal of Product Innovation Management, 39*(1), 66–94.

Kyriakopoulos, N., Kim, E., Hultink, E. J., & Santema, S. (2025). The impact of design thinking and artificial intelligence capabilities on performance: The role of new product development decision-making agility. *Journal of Business Research, 200*. https://doi.org/10.1016/j.jbusres.2025.115633

Lee, H. (2020). Role of artificial intelligence and enterprise risk management to promote corporate entrepreneurship and business performance: Evidence from Korean banking sector. *Journal of Intelligent & Fuzzy Systems, 39*(4), 5369–5386.

Li, Q., Liu, Q., Jiang, M., & Wang, R. (2024b). Virtual reality as a bridge: Enhancing intercultural learning and communication skills among international students. *International Communication of Chinese Culture, 11*(3), 385–411.

Li, X., Yang, G., Shao, T., Yang, D., & Liu, Z. (2024a). Does digital infrastructure promote individual entrepreneurship? Evidence from a quasi-natural experiment on the "broadband China" strategy. *Technological Forecasting and Social Change, 206*. https://doi.org/10.1016/j.techfore.2024.123555

Lin, C.-Y., Chau, K. Y., & Moslehpour, M. (2024). Bridging the Gap: The Nexus of Sustainability Innovation, Knowledge Sharing, and Green Volunteerism for Manufacturing Entrepreneurial Triumph. *Journal of Innovation & Knowledge, 9*(4), 100570. https://doi.org/10.1016/j.jik.2024.100570

Liu, Y., Kamal, M. M., Zhang, J. Z., Rahman, M., & Aydin, E. (2025). Leveraging digital crowdfunding platforms for SME sustainability in emerging markets: The roles of entrepreneurial competency, social capital, and supply chain trust. *Technovation, 147*. https://doi.org/10.1016/j.technovation.2025.103309

Magistretti, S., Ardito, L., & Petruzzelli, A. M. (2021). Framing the microfoundations of design thinking as a dynamic capability for innovation: Reconciling theory and practice. *Journal of Product Innovation Management, 38*(6), 645–667.

Mahato, S. S., Phi, G. T., & Prats, L. (2021). Design thinking for social innovation: Secrets to success for tourism social entrepreneurs. *Journal of Hospitality and Tourism Management, 49*, 396–406.

Martín-Rojas, R., Garrido-Moreno, A., & García-Morales, V. J. (2023). Social media use, corporate entrepreneurship and organizational resilience: A recipe for SMEs success in a post-Covid scenario. *Technological Forecasting and Social Change, 190*. https://doi.org/10.1016/j.techfore.2023.122421

Meier, A., & Kock, A. (2024). Agile R&D units' organisation and its relationship with innovation performance. *R&D Management, 54*(3), 496–512.

Nevi, G., Montera, R., Cucari, N., & Laviola, F. (2025). Integrating AI and ESG in digital platforms: New profiles of platform-based business models. *Journal of Engineering and Technology Management, 78*. https://doi.org/10.1016/j.jengtecman.2025.101913

Papadopoulos, T., Gunasekaran, A., Dubey, R., Altay, N., Childe, S. J., & Fosso-Wamba, S. (2017). The role of big data in explaining disaster resilience in supply chains for sustainability. *Journal of Cleaner Production, 142*, 1108–1118.

Parker, G., Van Alstyne, M., & Jiang, X. (2017). Platform ecosystems. *MIS Quarterly, 41*(1), 255–266.

Rajagopal. (2019). *Transgenerational marketing: Evolution, expansion, and experience.* Palgrave Macmillan.

Rajagopal. (2021). *Crowd-based business models - Using collective intelligence for market competitiveness.* Palgrave Macmillan.

Rajagopal. (2025). *Virtual engagement: Managing seamless marketing with technology.* Business Expert Press.

Remco, V., Jongen, M., & Zwetsloot, G. (2008). Business-driven innovations: Towards more sustainable chemical products. *Journal of Cleaner Production, 16*(S1), S85–S94.

Rajagopal. (2026). *Humanizing digital experience: Converging cognitive ergonomics and technology growth in marketing.* Business Expert Press. (in press).

Rajagopal, & Rajagopal, A. (2023). 'Seeing is experiencing': Impact of showcasing fashion merchandises on digital platforms. *Qualitative Market Research, 26*(3), 214–231.

Sestino, A., Santarelli, I., & Amatulli, C. (2022). *Infusing new technologies and luxury: A literature review and current issues on luxury fashion, food, and tourism.* In R. Pettinger, B. Gupta, A. Roja, & D. Cozmiuc (Eds.), *Handbook of Research on Digital Transformation Management and Tools* (pp. 474–488).

Szopinski, D., Schoormann, T., John, T., Knackstedt, R., & Kundish, D. (2020). Software tools for business model innovation: Current state and future challenges. *Enterprise Markets, 30*(3), 469–494.

Tiwary, N. K., Kumar, R. K., Sarraf, S., Kumar, P., & Rana, N. P. (2021). Impact assessment of social media usage in B2B marketing: A review of the literature and a way forward. *Journal of Business Research, 131*, 121–139.

Tukamuhabwa, B. R., Stevenson, M., Busby, J., & Zorzini, M. (2015). Supply chain resilience: Definition, review and theoretical foundations. *International Journal of Production Research, 53*(18), 5592–5623.

Wang, B. (2023, in press). Is Walmart the same as ten years ago? A non-parametric difference-in-differences analysis of Walmart development. *Regional Science and Urban Economics, 99*. https://doi.org/10.1016/j.regsciurbeco.2022.103863

Yin, Z., Gong, X., Guo, P., & Wu, T. (2019). What drives entrepreneurship in digital economy? Evidence from China. *Economic Modelling, 82*, 66–73.

PART III

Navigation Ahead

CHAPTER 6

Navigating the Future

Technology Transition and Transformation

There are emerging prospects and challenges in navigating the future cyberspace, which demonstrates multifaceted tasks across omnipresent information outlets contributing to meta knowledge of the society, industry, and cyber-human interface. Navigating the future cyberspace requires democratic cyberlaws, robust security measures, agility in knowledge, and lean strategies with strong governance. The changing attribute of cyberspace focuses on integration of responsible Artificial Intelligence (AI) to foster public-private collaboration for developing cyber resilience and governance frameworks. The probable threats in surfing future cyberspace are critical due to the threats of quantum computing and post-quantum cryptography, which significantly affect the information drain and security breach with increasingly complex and interconnected digital environments like hyper Internet of things (IoT). In view of the complexity of digital environments in the future, entrepreneurs and firms need to integrate AI tools for threat detection besides information analytics and predictive functions. Consequently, it is necessary to ensure convergence of diverse information processing techniques and test both verbal and non-verbal data models for secured navigation in the future. Strengthening cyber resilience demands adopting new security protocols to make safe

Rajagopal, A. Rajagopal, *Artificial Intelligence and Entrepreneurship*, Palgrave Studies of Entrepreneurship and Social Challenges in Developing Economies,
https://doi.org/10.1007/978-3-032-14904-6_6

transition of information from quantum computers based on advanced technology that uses complex algorithms like Qubits, super positioning, cause and effect interface, and protecting data from decoherence (Ahvanooey et al., 2025). The quantum computation is used in simulating molecular interactions in drug discovery, material science, AI and machine learning (ML), financial modeling, logistics, and to meet the challenges of cybersecurity.

Transiting from Web 2.0 to Web 3.0 has fostered intelligent infrastructure to manage complex computing scenarios. Such transition has leveraged both generative and predictive AI, blockchain technology, and token-based economies, and paved path for quantum computing. With the advancement of information and communication technology, the information openness has enabled entrepreneurs to rely on centralized networks and servers (cloud environment) to analyze cyber information in design thinking, manufacturing, operations, and success management underpinning the navigation on secured cyber infrastructures. As Web 3.0 matures in the future, the power of cyber information will become stronger and comprehensive, enabling wide range of enterprises to adapt to Web 3.0 on entrepreneurial platforms to enhance the significance of information analytics and integrating the real time data into the business to create value (Momtaz, 2022). The future perspective of entrepreneurial adaptation to cyber information is expected to leap from IoT to Internet-of-everything (IoE) ecosystem in the post-quantum computing era. However, in the current context, IoE is a conceptual network connecting smart things (entities), people, data, and processes to support intelligent decision-making to enhance user experiences in cyberspace. The future cyber ecosystem can be equipped with digital attributes and linked to smart machines, processes, and services to improve compatible decision-making through IoE network. It requires Internet-of-everything architecture with secured hardware and software protocols to defeat the cyber-attacks and override the vulnerability of cloud ecosystem to disseminate information and services through effective design and security protocols (Joseph et al., 2022). Consequently, the future of cyberspace is for the people to access, and its life stays beyond as people will inhabit it.

Broadly IoE interconnects people, processes, and performance by analyzing real time data to create intelligent responsive systems to resolve individual and social problems across geo-demographic segments and complex ecosystems. Technology-oriented countries benefit from IoE process in managing smart cities by focusing on Internet-based traffic management systems through cameras, sensors, and real time data analytics to optimize traffic conditions and reduce congestion in traffic flow. In addition, IoE reliance helps in managing smart lighting by programming illumination features and energy saving goals. The healthcare sector has been highly benefitted by connecting remote services with IoE devices and tools to monitor movements of patients remotely and analyzing real time data to make decisions. These cyber technology features have been extended also to manage smart ambulances by monitoring the real time emergency response, AI assisted diagnosis, and conducting robotic surgeries remotely. The industrial and manufacturing processes can be connected with IoE tools and platforms for predictive maintenance, resolving supply chain issues (tracking inventory and logistics management), and streamlining production through robotics and process automation. The bottom-line benefits of IoE tools and platforms witness improving the home and lifestyle, and customer experiences. Remotely managing devices like thermostats and electro domestic appliances, and monitoring mechanical, electrical, or human security breaches constitute major benefits toward home and lifestyle. Retailing management with IoE technology can help in maintaining smart shelves by detecting product levels, display visualization, and product replenishment. Personalized shopping by creating tailor made promotions and automated check outs based on sensors can be experienced.

The shape of future cyberspace, which entrepreneurs will witness, converge technologies in virtual environment with extended reality (XR) with immersive environments to organize workspace and social connects in three dimensional (3D) digital spaces. AI will act as both guide and gatekeeper in the XR environment providing core contents and mediating cross domain interaction (cyber technology-AI-human interface) to co-create experiences. The advanced cyber environment will support Web 3.0 technologies for entrepreneurs with decentralized infrastructure to enable user owned networks enabling ease-of-work, privacy, and autonomy. In addition, the quantum and edge computing will enhance hyper personalized experiences with high speed and security within the real time ecosystem (Wang & Wang, 2022). One of the core attributes of futuristic cyberspace is to provide digital identity and platforms for multifaceted tasks in different contexts comprising professional, social, and creative work targets. Creative entrepreneurs can develop their digital identity and omnipresence through digital repetition systems with trust scores, verified skills, and community endorsement on digital platforms (Fang et al.,

2023). The self-sovereign identity system will allow the users to control data and credentials within their domain to observe secured growth with creativity and privacy. The existing cyberspace lacks efficient e-governance policies to accommodate creativity and intangible assets within IoE environment. Therefore, cybersecurity practices need proactive transformations to develop security guidelines and implement working with future digital channels (Kane et al., 2009).

Extended reality encompasses virtual reality (VR), augmented reality (AR), and mixed reality (MR) technology as an advancement of cyber technology in the changing cyberspace. VR technology is used in gaming, virtual labs in education, healthcare, and design and architecture, while the digital element of AR connects with real world through electronic devices like smartphone or AR glasses. Creative companies like IKEA use AR to visualize home furniture and ergonomic home design whereas the practical application of navigation can be witnessed on live views of google maps in a global context. MR combines both AR and VR technologies which allows interactions between both real and virtual objects. MR is extensively used in simulating manufacturing and maintenance needs in industries and remotely collaborates through the 3D models in a real time situation across locations. In addition, MR is extensively used in healthcare for medical visualization during surgical procedures to visualize the problem areas and the status of internal organs.

A hybrid conversational-communication style drives positive customer-brand relationships and helps firms to evaluate the geodemographic association of brands with the consumers. Firms can develop proximity index based on communication, interactivity, cognitive variables, relationship drivers, competitive touchpoints, and business growth. In addition, co-creating customer service and relationship hubs fosters marketing, public relations, and communications strategies to develop a positive consumer-business helix and ecosystem. AI has emerged as a new facet of information technology, which has overpowered the conventional practices of managerial and organizational cognition (Helfat & Martin, 2015). Generative AI is a recent outgrowth of crowd-based Artificial Intelligence, which is commonly used in the managerial decision-making process. Consequently, both Artificial Intelligence and knowledge management can be perceived as strategic enablers of managerial and organizational cognition, which contribute to collaborative learning and developing repositories of metaknowledge diffused through management networks in new generation organizations. Generative AI is an innovative phase that serves as a next generation intelligent agent in developing knowledge management repositories in an organization to support managerial decisions (Rajagopal, 2025).

In the existing cyber ecosystem, start-up e-commerce companies or a group of e-commerce companies may choose to share hosting of the web server with the principal server of the mother company. However, Virtual Private Server (VPS) provides better control over the data exchanges in business and resources as compared to the shared hosting for single client firms. Beyond the options discussed above, a dedicated server offers maximum control and resources, which is ideal for large e-commerce sites with heavy traffic. Another option for the web server is cloud hosting, which is both scalable and flexible, allowing firms to adjust resources based on demand and manage fluctuations in traffic and transactions. While setting up the web server for e-commerce, most firms face a major challenge to prioritize securities to safely handle sensitive customer data and protect the personal data from security breach and cyber-attacks (Leone et al., 2021). Implementing SSL certificates, firewalls, and regular security updates, using secured payment gateways, and complying with industry standards like Payment Card Industry Data Security Standard (PCI-DSS), data can be largely protected. PCI-DSS is a set of security standards designed to ensure that all e-commerce firms who accept, process, store, or transmit credit card information maintain a secure environment. This security measure helps in encrypting the transmission of cardholder data across open public networks. In addition to securing the electronic payment processes, firms also need to strengthen the inventory management system to track stock levels, manage orders, and optimize warehouse operations. Efficient inventory management is essential for meeting customer demand and minimizing costs. The shipping and fulfillment solutions manage the logistics of delivering products to customers. These solutions integrate with various carriers and provide real-time tracking to ensure timely and accurate deliveries (Rajagopal, 2025).

Cyberspace Ahead

As cyberspace continues to evolve in I-3 dimensions comprising immersive, intelligent, and interconnect domains, AI and large language modeling (LLM) are growing as a cyber neural network to shape the future cyberspace. The infrastructure for future cyberspace is largely designed with AI and LLM to manage cloud resources, real time optimization, and routing information through autonomous systems and through smart agents, which assist in navigating complex digital ecosystems from virtual scenarios to de-centralized and customized platforms. Such infrastructural setting will be helpful for entrepreneurs to develop technology-based designs to gain competitive advantage through customized AI and ML platforms. Such infrastructure will elevate adaptive interfaces to enhance personalized experience based on AI-human interface behavior, emotions, and process contextualities. LLM modeling contributes to building the interface layer of cyber infrastructure by translating human behavior, intents, and attributes into machine-executable actions on ML platforms to facilitate conversational interface and synthesizing knowledge. The extensive involvement of AI and ML will generate new cognitive ecosystems to provide space for the co-evolution of AI, LLM, and human cognition. Such technological advancement will facilitate collective and co-intelligence in future entrepreneurial decision-making by adapting to techno-social changes (Lyu & Wu, 2023).

Cognitive ecosystems in the context of changing cyber scenarios refers to dynamic and interconnected environment, which allows the AI and digital systems to co-evolve with human intelligence. Entrepreneurs engaged with technology-based designing and entrepreneurial processes will be able to develop contextual awareness on digital platforms to make decisions with collective intelligence. The AI-human collaboration enables entrepreneurs for seamless interaction among customers, stakeholders, key partners, and intelligent agents like LLM and autonomous system to develop shared problem solving, technology-based creativity, and decision-making. The cognitive ecosystems provide contextual awareness on user behavior, emotions, and responses through sensor inputs to adapt to AI responses in real time. One of the major changes in working with future cyberspace infrastructure is about managing distributed intelligence across humans, devices, platforms, and AI agents. Working under such scenario allows entrepreneurs to upscale their business through resilient systems by learning from interactions, feedback, and dynamic real time conditions (Wu et al., 2025).

Most global companies have integrated generative and predictive AI into their business operations into embedded tools of cloud environment such as OpenAI and Anthropic, navigating a different ecosystem with faster information transition and logical appropriation to develop competitive AI infrastructure. The advanced AI infrastructure is based on cost leadership in AI model development, customization, and calibration to manage real time scenarios with generative and predictive AI and ML for data analytics. The futuristic AI solutions provide a roadmap for adopting a dual track approach to experience operational efficiency and advanced strategic outcomes (Joshi et al., 2025). The dual track approach in AI for business accommodates parallel strategies to drive operational efficiency and strategic (long-term) transformative innovation to integrate AI landscape for real time competitive advantage in business. The operational efficiency is a combination of AI-ML integration to enhance productivity and minimize CTR factors with improved accuracy. Such integration helps in automating repetitive tasks, optimizing supply chains, and enhancing customer experience by creating tangible and near-term efficiencies. The transformative innovation strategy enables AI-synchronized new product development process and customization in agile environments to gain competitive differentiation.

The future of cyberspace is expected to mark deeper integration with physical-cyber reality through IoE, AR, VR, and MR applications. Smart cities, auto pilot vehicles, and intelligent infrastructure will have seamless connectivity and real time data exchange to develop omnipresent contents to be disseminated through cloud environment for synchronous decision-making. AI will play key role in reshaping cyberspace with personalized digital assistants and predictive data analysis to enhance immersive experience and enlisting several options for decision-making based on complex algorithmic models and robust governance frameworks. The decentralization and expansion of Web 3.0 applications will shift controls from centralized servers to user-based servers democratizing the digital services and reducing reliance on centralized digital service providers. Such decentralization and user-based ownership will improve the scalability of business operations within the regulatory frameworks. However, the major challenges in ethical and social implications need to be addressed collectively to reduce the stress from cyberattacks and AI-Human interface. With the advancement of information and communication technology, AI and ML robust combination, the future cyberspace can be identified beyond technological domain as a human assistant with embedded cognitive values and emotions.

AI in Development Sectors

AI is used as one of the technological advancements in various development sectors, primarily agriculture, health, and sustainability, including transportation, renewable energy, and waste management, in convergence with the Sustainable Development Goals (SDGs). Entrepreneurs can explore business development opportunities using AI and ML tools in the vulnerable social sectors as stated above by automating the routine tasks to manage complex development scenarios by analyzing real-time data to enhance decision-making and resource allocation. Entrepreneurship in sectoral development is potentially supported by AI and ML tools to provide solutions in complex scenarios and enable entrepreneurs in analyzing both verbal and non-verbal data to support both tactical and strategic decision-making in health, agriculture, and sustainability sectors. AI-powered tools provide comprehensive information support with accuracy in managing complex social health scenarios such as disease detection and diagnosis, which encourage entrepreneurs to take creative steps in social entrepreneurship by analyzing health-related data, patients record, and healthcare images using AI tools. Social health entrepreneurship can provide comprehensive information support through AI and ML platforms to enable healthcare professionals in disease diagnosis more accurately by geo-demographic segments to plan controlled healthcare support for social disease control and prevention. Healthcare entrepreneurs can serve as information hub for epidemic prediction to track the infectious diseases by using geo-demographic data provided by AI to collaborate with health workers in reducing the risk of potential outbreaks, resource distribution, and resource planning. Social enterprises using AI can also provide information on the availability of healthcare professionals and collaborate with hospitals in optimizing the bed occupancy, availability of emergency rooms and operation theaters, and availability of ambulances for emergency transportation.

Agricultural entrepreneurship with a focus on technology largely relies on AI and ML tools to guide precision farming by training farmers in optimization of irrigation, fertilization, monitoring plant protection and crop diseases, and increasing productivity through data-driven insights. AI also helps agricultural entrepreneurs in crop rotation prospects and yield management through resource mapping, food security measures, and indicating the crop-risk zones. Agricultural entrepreneurs also use AI-powered predictive models to help farmers and communities prepare for weather extremities by climate modeling using AI and ML to map weather patterns, climate adaptation, and crop resilience models. These entrepreneurs largely serve as agribusiness centers and educate farmers using AI and ML tools that provide satellite imagery and acoustic sensors for crop protection from animals and unforeseen conditions. Agricultural enterprises support member farmers within the community with AI-powered drones and sensors to monitor crop health, soil conditions, crop epidemics, and mapping yield patterns, besides connecting farmers with agricultural markets through AI platforms.

Enterprises working with environment and sustainability goals use AI and ML platforms for climate modeling, climate prediction, and design mitigation strategies by analyzing the chronological climate data. In addition, ML analyzes wildlife conservation through camera images and acoustic data, besides pollution control by tracking air and water quality and suggesting needful interventions. AI analyzes large databases to encourage evidence-based policy designing and implementation through AI assistants by maintaining transparency and accountability in public systems. The major challenges in using AI and ML in sectoral entrepreneurial activities are primarily data privacy and security, accessibility to AI and ML platforms, and the digital divide across geodemographic segments. The digital divide indicates the accessibility to AI-based information and the availability of technology in public domains. Broadly, AI tools and ML platforms are considered as powerful enablers of sectoral development that offer scalable solutions with inclusive policies and robust governance.

Large companies follow resource-based business models in the social and environmental development sectors, which are based on exploitation of natural resources such as agriculture, water harvesting, and energy production. These resources are regulated by the state authorities; however, some resources of commons that are used in collective production (agriculture, water management, and community housing) are controlled by social organizations. However, one of the criticisms of traditional economy-based business models is the exclusive focus on resource allocation, ignoring societal well-being and the impact of revenue-generating projects on biological ecosystems. The unstable rate of consumption of natural resources needs to be controlled for prolonged conservation of resources for continuous production activities. Therefore, the development of new (economic) systems with an emphasis on sustainable practices, technologies, and processes has become necessary at the bottom-of-the-pyramid geo-demographic segments (Bocken et al., 2014).

Multidimensional growth of marketing organization is best understood as the next step in the evolution from a resource-centric business model to a customer-centric knowledge-sharing model (Rajagopal, 2021).

Public policies exhibit global-local concerns and delineate funding programs and social benefits within the political ideology. The government emphasizes implementation of Sustainable Development Goals (SDGs) at the grassroots. Most companies design and implement sustainable projects in various sectors as corporate social responsibilities. Firms encourage stakeholder engagement in sustainable production and use of technology in key sectors like agriculture, energy, water conservation, and food products manufacturing. Business modeling for sustainable products largely focuses on both business-to-consumers and business-to-business activities (Rajagopal, 2021). The AI-based information enables marketing strategies to be developed around 11Ps as detailed below:

- Product—sustainable, organic, attractive, innovation, social need-based, utilitarian
- Price—affordable, competitive
- Place—availability, backward and forward logistics, niche markets, proximity
- Promotion—diet concept, social value, value and lifestyle, ethnicity, anthropomorphic perceptions, endorsements
- Packaging—sustainable, green effect, circular economy based, recycled
- Pace—first mover advantage, psycho-social standing, top-of-the-mind memory
- People—consumer education, customer advocacy, motivators, gatekeepers, community, and family
- Performance—success stories, visual information, evidence-based marketing
- Psychodynamics—social networks, interpersonal communication, digital forums
- Posture—social values, social branding, sustainability, people, global values
- Proliferation—diversification in sustainability activities

Sustainability projects are designed with a participatory research approach by understanding the needs of the stakeholders at the local level. These projects are aimed at reducing the negative impacts of environmentally ineffective industries within the region and increasing the positive benefits on ecology in all production sectors like agriculture, irrigation, silviculture, sericulture, pisciculture, apiculture, and renewable energy production. These projects are central to the stockholder welfare and socio-economic benefits within the niche. Community-based natural resources management has been encouraged by the social organizations (self-help groups and non-governmental organizations) on the assumption that the decision-making process in natural resource management is a collective process within the communities and among stakeholders. This community approach has not only fostered knowledge and commitment among the stakeholders but also stimulated ecological innovation in start-up enterprises at the local level (Rajagopal, 2021). However, commercialization of frugal and reverse innovations in the green economic and industrial sector is a major challenge. The problem of commercialization of innovation is largely attributed to the interface of top-down (public policies and funding) and bottom-up approaches (social and entrepreneurial governance), which primarily involves the inter-institutional arrangements to diffuse and market the innovations (Armitage, 2005; Rajagopal, 2021).

Social Technology and AI

Social entrepreneurship relies on social technology and AI as two transformative forces connecting people to communicate and collaborate in entrepreneurial activities. Broadly, social technology refers to digital platforms and tools driven by AI and ML to facilitate human interaction and collaborative entrepreneurial workspaces. AI and ML serve as enablers to simulate human intelligence, database learning process, and content management in developing entrepreneurial business. Social technology can also be classified as digital communication networks, which not only connect people but also enable AI to predict social behavior such as consumption patterns and market trends. The AI-supported market information and behavioral analysis guide entrepreneurs in making appropriate business models by integrating AI and ML into social technology. The convergence of social technology and AI provides opportunity to entrepreneurs in personalization and adapting to AI-suggested contents to develop a market fit of entrepreneurial business models. One of the major advantages of social technology and AI in entrepreneurial business is toward analyzing social media content and curating feeds to match entrepreneurial product and service designs, consumer preferences, and collaborative engagements with users, stakeholders, and business partners in developing demand-centric innovative products.

Design thinking can be a critical facilitator of new technologies, but it is also a technology in its own right—a social technology that encourages more productive innovation conversations that are strategically valuable for dynamic capability building. By overcoming social and psychological barriers in innovation processes, design thinking accelerates progress on critical imperatives: allowing innovators at all levels to sense new opportunities; seize them by overcoming cognitive biases and aligning stakeholders; and transform and reconfigure resources. It accomplishes this through a set of well-recognized practices (Liedtka, 2020). In fact, recognizing and responding to human irrationality underlies many popular management approaches, from design thinking to Agile Software Development, Lean Start-up, and choice architecture. In the strategy field, behavioral strategy and strategy-as-practice perspectives call attention to the essential role of human actors in capability building. A shared premise of these approaches is that while attempting to predict or control human conduct is hazardous, behavior can be anticipated and shaped to the mutual advantage of humans, their organizations, and society (Organ et al., 2022).

AI-powered virtual assistants and chatbots significantly support technology-based micro, small, and medium enterprises to facilitate customer services, community campaign management, and generate psychodynamics based on content analysis generated by AI. The real-time assistance provided by AI and ML simulates human conversation through AI agents, chatbots, and virtual assistants to make appropriate human intervention in resolving complex scenarios of consumers and providing value appropriate solutions. The sentiment and trend analysis provided by AI can guide entrepreneurs to measure the crowd behavior, social trends, and public sentiment by identifying critical behavioral factors and developing compatibility of entrepreneurial operations to emerging market trends. However, entrepreneurs may face anomalies in following AI suggestions, as the behavioral analysis provided by AI may amplify societal biases, leading to exclusion of certain groups and creating bias and social anxiety. Broadly, the intersection of social technology and AI enables entrepreneurs to reshape the digital landscape and explore customer-centric opportunities by developing innovative products and services to cater to existing demand. Accordingly, AI empowers the entrepreneurial design process by engaging users, stakeholders, and business partners in analyzing behavioral contents to develop an enterprise-market fit.

The social challenges broadly include technologies to support low-cost renewable energy, green housing, farming operations, and public health management. The social connectivity and collective intelligence-driven technology development support innovations to be used at community commons to meet the social challenges. The involvement of technology developers with society is an important consideration to understand the problems, needs, and probable solutions for stakeholders within the given demographic attributes. The stakeholder preferences on technology-based solutions help in designing and developing affordable technologies at the grassroots. The involvement of stakeholders, therefore, strengthens the process of design thinking through user insights. Community involvement, technology co-creation, and user insights foster the social acceptance of technology through perceived use value and ease-of-use perceptions of stakeholders. The user insights in technology transfer to the stakeholder inspire all categories of users, including lead users, early adopters, early majority, and late majority, except laggards. However, the technological attributes determine the cost of technology and its lifecycle, which affect the social entrepreneurship and stakeholder engagement. Commonly, social technologies address the triple bottom line, embedding people (stakeholders), planet (sustainability), and profit (social payoff). The governance of social technology can be well managed by the stakeholders with adequate knowledge and experience (Rajagopal, 2014). Therefore, adequate knowledge and skills should be imparted to the technology governance teams. Transfer of social technologies requires need-based user alignment and articulation to manage its applications, which will help diffusion and adaptation of technology.

AI and frugal innovation are symbiotic to affordable product development to enhance the proximity of consumers for low-cost innovative products. Frugal innovation combined with AI are two powerful forces interacting to shape entrepreneurial development with changing technology. AI represents the cutting-edge digital designing and manufacturing platforms, computational intelligence, and low-cost solutions to create simple, affordable, and trendy solutions, overriding the resource-constrained entrepreneurial ecosystem. The AI and frugal innovation offer opportunities to understand consumer behavior and access intelligent technology to drive inclusive growth and innovation embedding sustainability. The low-cost solutions provided by micro, small, and medium enterprises are developed with minimal infrastructure, limited materials, energy, and capital. However, the AI-driven frugal innovative product designs are social- and market-context sensitive, customized to serve the local needs by understanding problem, needs, and solutions (PNS) factors. Frugal innovative products supported by AI and ML platforms have attributes of digital intelligence, adaptability, and scalability to low-cost solutions in various social sectors, including smart diagnostics in healthcare, agricultural optimization, microfinance and financial inclusion, and disaster management. AI-powered small enterprises support local healthcare systems by analyzing images and regulating the mobile devices in remote areas. Enterprises using AI models support small-scale farmers in optimizing AI-controlled irrigation and detecting crop diseases and weather patterns using smartphone applications.

Broadly, social technology addresses the social and psychological aspects of innovation, which often helps decision-makers to make choices driven primarily by analyzing the prevailing problems, needs, and expected solutions. Since start-up technologies possess a mindset that prefers to develop low-cost technology platforms to seize opportunity, they tend to drive social action by understanding the PNS factors of stakeholders. Thus, significant collective intelligence and participatory research in the community are encouraging tools to undertake experimentation-based learning in action. Increasing confidence and a sense of economic growth within the communities by adapting to new technologies has significantly encouraged the social innovation process and has fostered new mindsets and behaviors. Therefore, social technology today provides a set of knowledge to drive entrepreneurship, scalable tools, and methods to expedite, in a human-centered way to drive continuous innovation. Digital technology also brings a social technology capable of facilitating the development of dynamic capabilities needed to meet the challenges of adaptation and innovation in a VUCA (volatility, uncertainty, complexity, and ambiguity) environment, where both innovation and technology demand continuous improvement. Despite the potential of AI, integrating AI into entrepreneurial activities faces challenges in data security, infrastructure gaps, ethical concerns, and periodical capacity building to update AI and ML knowledge. Many low-resource entrepreneurial environments face difficulty in accessing data to customize effective AI models due to the quality of Internet services, accessibility, and quality of energy supply. In addition, entrepreneurs require periodical training and support to maintain AI-enabled solutions within the existing low-resource settings.

The digital technology (DT) has been helpful to innovators and technology developers to embed new ways to augment the perceived use of technology and produce higher quality solutions more likely to receive user acceptance. The emphasis on co-creation of innovation and managing innovation business projects in partnership with the local companies is gradually generating technological breakthroughs, allowing emerging companies to reduce the time to bring innovative products and services to market. The recent trend of carrying out innovation in the business-to-consumer and business-to-business segments by companies exhibits different ways of deploying price and volume advantages in global competition. Large companies practice outsourcing innovation, collaborating with start-up enterprises, investing in open innovation, and engaging in driving public-private partnerships (Rajagopal, 2021). In the evolving landscape of digital innovations, user-driven AI in technology emphasizes co-creation, customization, and social responsiveness in developing meaningful solutions contextual to PNS factors. User-driven AI can be trained to fit user behavior by understanding feedback loops and AI-human collaboration. User-driven AI can be developed by entrepreneurs through personalized applications in healthcare, as patients can track symptoms, receive alerts, and participate in clinical dialogues through AI-powered health apps and digital platforms. Future AI technology identified as Explainable AI (XAI) intends to help users in understanding the process of decision-making and guide human behavior through human-in-the-loops (HITL) systems. HITL represents a hybrid approach engaging humans to actively participate in learning operations and refinement of AI models by validating real-time decision-making, feedback, compliance, and refinement. HITL systems offer a balanced approach to automation by leveraging the speed of information pooling, classification, and analysis to support decision-making.

The user-driven technology developed by appropriately analyzing social problems and determining contextual needs serves stakeholders as congruent with the PNS factors. Often, social technologies are developed under public policy programs in developing countries and are fostered by technological alliances with large companies. Global-local alliances have been effective in developing countries for the development of specific sectors such as health, housing, and farming. Social technologies are commonly tested for collective solutions in the social laboratories. Most social technologies are developed through the project management approach using DMAIC (define, measure, analyze, implement, and control), CTQ (critical to quality), and QFD (quality function deployment) tools (Rajagopal, 2021). Such technologies and supporting infrastructure are developed in congruence with the stakeholder preferences to gain confidence in society. In delivering social technologies, one of the major challenges is about determining the ownership and local governance. It requires social leaders to ensure people's engagement in the technology development process and build trust among the stakeholders. The economics of social technology is largely determined by analyzing the proportionate triadic effects of CTR (cost, time, and risk) and CBP (cost, benefit, and profit). Accordingly, the socio-technical system plays a critical role in developing and delivering social technologies by understanding the social structures, design of systems, and applications thereof (Suarez et al., 2018).

Innovation entrepreneurship is a convergence of start-up enterprises and the sponsoring companies, which moves from the stage of initiation to systematic project management to commercialization, and finally developing sustainable innovation through incremental innovations. Companies need to invest substantial resources toward consumer education in order to create consumer demand. Besides, they must carry out product demonstrations such as 'do-it-yourself' and adaptive customization by allowing consumers to use the new products for a reasonable period and perceive value for money associated with the products. However, the opportunities for open innovation, incremental innovation, and enhancement of the use value of innovative products over the stages of the product life cycle finally take the innovation business projects to the initiation stage of the next generation innovative products. Incubation of innovations has emerged as a new model of start-up facilitation in most developing economies. Venture capitalists review the incubators and assess the projected growth and profitability in businesses to invest. They review the incubators to diversify risky investment portfolios, while the prospective entrepreneurs approach the incubators to review the economically viable and technologically feasible support for start-up projects. Entrepreneurial incubators face both challenges and opportunities to grow into competitive enterprises considering the embedded investment and entrepreneurial risks. Broadly, there are five incubator archetypes such as the university incubator, the independent commercial incubator, the regional business incubator, the company-internal incubator, and the virtual incubator (Beckman et al., 2018). An innovation breakthrough in firms can deliver a strong advantage to the overall posture of the company in the marketplace and drive a major shift in industry leadership. However, not all companies show the ability to foster management innovation due to a lack of generating unique ideas. A management innovation creates long-lasting advantage if it is based on a novel principle that challenges traditional wisdom, is systemic in processes and methods, and is supported by a program of the company to carry out innovation.

Transformational Entrepreneurship and AI

The digital entrepreneurial landscape has been significantly driven by AI, which enables smart decision-making, automating entrepreneurial operations, and enhancing customer engagement to develop value-based enterprises. Most enterprises use AI to build scalable, efficient, and innovative ventures to stay competitive in the marketplace. Zendesk, a Danish company founded in 2007 with its headquarters in San Francisco, offers a comprehensive suite of AI products and features designed to automate customer service to enhance client productivity and customized customer experience. Zendesk AI agents are autonomous conversational bots, which manage a large volume of customer interactions to resolve complex issues across digital channels and e-commerce web portals. These agents provide omnichannel support and require zero training, as most advanced AI agents can be launched without extensive upfront training in managing business scenarios.

The AI content personalization has also been experienced by Netflix, which employs machine learning algorithms to analyze user behavior and recommend personalized contents. The AI-driven approach of Netflix has significantly boosted user engagement, which supported AI in pooling information, providing sentiment analysis, and identifying the negative behavior of users (analysis, feedback, and product dropouts). The AI-driven analysis and suggestions have significantly contributed to the content selection, duration of entertainment products, and classifications based on user feedback. The contribution of AI to content personalization and content formulation has significantly contributed to the global expansion and success of Netflix digital entertainment company. AI is extensively used by Netflix in content creation and production by analyzing trends and predicting competitive content across entertainment channels from the perspective of the viewers' interests and behavioral disposition. Netflix also leverages generative AI for visual effects and to seek guidance in creative production for the expected success of the program. AI also helps in optimizing video quality and reducing buffering time by adjusting the Internet speed with the quality of the stream. The content localization by understanding geo-demographic behavior of viewers to produce entertainment programs is a good fit for local streaming. AI is also used extensively for automatic translation, insertion of subtitles, and dubbing in different languages for global audiences.

Reliance retail is an upcoming business segment of the Reliance group of industry in India, which uses AI tools and ML platforms for demand forecasting, supply chain optimization, and behavioral analysis of consumers to learn the PNS factors and the shopping experience. The retail-specific applications of AI and ML are part of the parent company Reliance Industries Limited, which has launched a technology subsidiary as Reliance Intelligence and is building AI-Ready infrastructure with global partners like Google and Meta. The AI applications in Reliance Retail include analyzing customer experience, supply chain management, and retail operations. The major challenges in analyzing customer experiences are the dynamic preferences and behavior of customers, which are often influenced by the competing brands. AI analyzes customer preferences and shopping behavior to provide curated product recommendations and organized contents for targeted promotions. Consequently, AI paves the path for the customer journey across various platforms including digital channels like JioMart and Ajio. The virtual assistants of AI are extensively used by the company in promoting its retail beauty brands through AI-driven virtual kiosks, which offer try-ons and personalized recommendations to customers based on their complexion, skin type, dermatological sensitivity, and need for a natural look. In addition, AI-powered chatbots and voice assistants provide instant customer support by responding to queries and assisting in purchases. 5G-powered Smart Mirrors in stores allow customers to virtually try-on clothing by enhancing in-store experience and refining brand choices. The AI-supported cameras are used in various points from farm to stores to assist the quality of agricultural and food products, track shelf life, optimize inventory handling, and reduce food waste. The real-time logistics are managed by AI systems to optimize last-mile delivery through predetermined routes. The company uses AI also to enhance post-purchase support enabling real-time tracking of extended services (deliveries and maintenance) and proactive service quality checks.

Myntra, a virtual fashion retail giant in India, uses AI and ML extensively to provide not only personalized shopping experience but also to optimize its supply chain and customer services in the Indian market. The company uses AI to deliver an intuitive shopping experience and address specific needs of online fashion retailing. The company uses personalized engines to analyze user browsing history, past purchases, and real-time trends through the AI-powered *My Stylist* featured application. Myntra has introduced natural language search in partnership with Microsoft and commissioned *MyFashionGPT*, which allows users to find products using queries via natural language processing. The generative AI also enables visual search by allowing users to upload an image and find look-alike items from its catalogue. In this process AI detects visual components like patterns, colors, and near-match products. The company has implemented an AR platform embedding virtual try-on features for beauty products and apparels. This helps users in achieving self-actualization and self-esteem while visualizing the try-on products on themselves. Specialized AI tools like skin analyzers help consumers in choosing appropriate products suitable for their skin attributes and social value. The AI for beauty analyzes consumer data through quiz-style inputs and algorithmic frameworks.

Hennes & Mauritz, commonly known as H&M, is a Swedish multinational retail company founded in 1947 for fast fashion products, fashion accessories, and homeware. H&M uses AI across its operations to improve efficiency in the retailing process, enhance customer experience, and achieve sustainability goals. The AI applications range from supply chain optimization to AI-powered forecasting and generating digital twin models for competitive marketing. The digital twin model was launched by the company in 2025 using AI to generate digital replicas of over 30 of its models to showcase products on social media and marketing campaigns. The digital twin models were subjected to ownership rights and received compensation for each use of their likeness. H&M largely depends on AI for faster and cost-effective content creation to generate verbal and non-verbal campaign features. This allows the company to adapt to creating specific localized market contents with new trends. The AI-powered virtual fitting rooms and digital avatars help online customers to visualize apparel-fit to their body structure. H&M uses AI-powered recycling to manage textile waste by fiber composition, which is critical to large-scale recycling and being proactive to the circular economy. Accordingly, the company has broader goals to move toward better, sustainable, and circular fashion modeling by reducing the reliance on non-green fibers.

References

Ahvanooey, M. T., Mazurczyk, W., Zhao, J., Caviglione, L., Choo, K.-K. J., Kilger, M., Conti, M., & Misoczki, R. (2025). Future of cyberspace: A critical review of standard security protocols in the post-quantum era. *Computer Science Review, 57*. https://doi.org/10.1016/j.cosrev.2025.100738

Armitage, D. (2005). Adaptive capacity and community-based natural resource management. *Environment Management, 35*(6), 703–715.

Beckman, S., Scott, S., & Wymore, L. (2018). Collaborative innovation: Exploring the intersections among theater, Art and Business in the Classroom. *Journal of Open Innovation: Technology, Market, and Complexity, 4*(4), 52. https://doi.org/10.3390/joitmc4040052

Bocken, N. M. P., Short, S. W., Rana, P., & Evans, S. (2014). A literature and practice review to develop sustainable business model archetypes. *Journal of Cleaner Production, 65*(1), 42–56.

Fang, H., Xiao, Z., Wang, X., Li, X., & Hanzo, L. (2023). Collaborative authentication for 6G networks: An edge intelligence based autonomous approach. *IEEE transactions information forensics security, 18*(2023), 2091–2103.

Helfat, E., & Martin, J. A. (2015). Dynamic managerial capabilities: Review and assessment of managerial impact on strategic change. *Journal of Management, 41*(5), 1281–1312.

Joseph, D., Misoczki, R., Manzano, M., Tricot, J., Pinuaga, F. D., Lacombe, O., Leichenauer, S., Hidary, J., Venables, P., & Hansen, R. (2022). Transitioning organizations to post-quantum cryptography. *Nature, 605*, 237–243.

Joshi, A., Greeven, M. J., Liu, S., & Li, K. (2025). How savvy companies are using Chinese AI. *Harvard Business Review*.

Kane, G. C., Fichman, R. G., Gallaugher, J., & Glaser, J. (2009). Community relations 2.0. *Harvard Business Review, 87*(11), 45–50.

Leone, D., Schiavone, F., Appio, F. P., & Chiao, B. (2021). How does artificial intelligence enable and enhance value co-creation in industrial markets? An exploratory case study in the healthcare ecosystem. *Journal of Business Research, 129*, 849–859.

Liedtka, J. (2020). Putting Technology in its Place: Design thinking's social Technology at Work. *California Management Review, 62*(2), 53–83.

Lyu, Y. G., & Wu, F. (2023). Toward a more general empowering artificial intelligence. *Engineering, 25*, 1–2.

Momtaz, P. P. (2022). Some very simple economics of web3 and the metaverse. *FinTech, 1*(3), 225–234.

Organ, J., O'Neill, S., & Shanahan, B. W. (2022). Development of social technology entrepreneurial ventures: A challenge project-based learning approach. *IFAC-Papers Online, 55*(39), 181–186.

Rajagopal. (2014). *Architecting Enterprise: Managing innovation, technology, and global competitiveness.* Palgrave Macmillan.

Rajagopal. (2021). *Sustainable businesses in developing economies - socio-economic and governance perspectives.* Palgrave Macmillan.

Rajagopal. (2025). *Virtual engagement: Managing seamless marketing with technology.* Business Exprert Press.

Suarez, F. F., Utterback, J., von, G. P., & Kang, H. Y. (2018). The hybrid trap: why most efforts to bridge old and new technology miss the mark MIT Sloan Management Review. https://sloanreview.mit.edu/article/the-hybrid-trap-why-most-efforts-to-bridge-old-and-new-technology-miss-the-mark/

Wang, Q., & Wang, D. (2022). Understanding failures in security proofs of multi-factor authentication for mobile devices. *IEEE Transactions on Information Forensics and Security, 18*, 597–612.

Wu, F., Shen, T., Bäck, T., Chen, J., Huang, G., Jin, Y., Kuang, K., Li, M., Lu, C., Miao, J., & Wang, Y. (2025). Knowledge-Empowered, Collaborative, and Co-Evolving AI Models: The Post-LLM Roadmap. *Engineering, 44*, 87–100. https://doi.org/10.1016/j.eng.2024.12.008

Index[1]

[1] Note: Page numbers followed by 'n' refer to notes.

Rajagopal, A. Rajagopal, *Artificial Intelligence and Entrepreneurship*, Palgrave Studies of Entrepreneurship and Social Challenges in Developing Economies,
https://doi.org/10.1007/978-3-032-14904-6

The manufacturer's authorised representative in the EU is Springer Nature Customer Service Centre GmbH, Europaplatz 3, 69115 Heidelberg, Germany. If you have any concerns regarding our products, please contact ProductSafety@springernature.com

Printed and bound by CPI Group (UK) Ltd, Croydon, CR0 4YY

16/09/2026

02217792-0007